ALL CHANGE HERE

NAOMI MITCHISON

All Change Here

Girlhood and Marriage

THE BODLEY HEAD
LONDON SYDNEY
TORONTO

© Naomi Mitchison 1975
Photographs © Naomi Mitchison 1975
ISBN 0 370 10485 4
Printed and bound in Great Britain for
The Bodley Head Ltd
9 Bow Street, London WC2E 7AL
by Unwin Brothers Limited
Old Woking, Surrey
Set in Monotype Imprint
First published 1975

CONTENTS

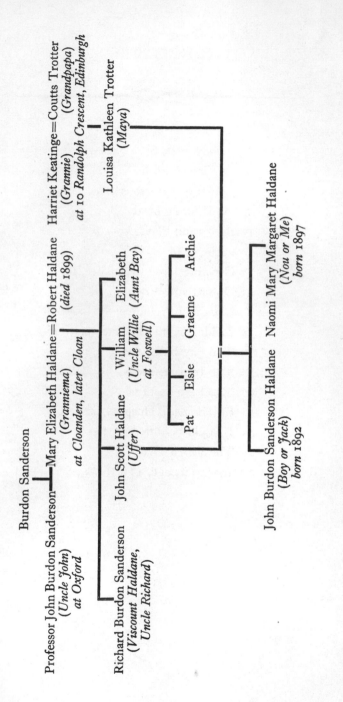

ILLUSTRATIONS

I

Boy into Girl

This book is, I am afraid, less factual and more self-centred than
its predecessor, *Small Talk*. It seems as though one's clear
memory of how things looked and smelled and sounded and
tasted, which goes back into childhood, gets twisted and obscured
with the coming of puberty. It is not one's self one looks back
on but a teenager or, as we said then, a flapper. What affinity
have I with this creature? I can fit quite well into the six-year-old,
not into the sixteen-year-old. As in the earlier book certain
things stand out, but often in a different way to how they did
when I was a child; where the child can be an individualist,
the essential thing for a teenager is to conform. So I must write
about myself as the perceiver, but largely the conformer, sometimes rebelling a bit, but never quite enough. Again, if I am to
be honest about a book of 'memories', I ought only to put in
what I can actually remember; and as one gets out of one's hard-
headed childhood with its factual curiosity about the adult world,
the main thing one remembers is one's self. So this book is not
so much social history, those taken-for-granted differences
which are so curious now; there is more about the development
of a writer and that is something which is perhaps of interest.
It begins in 1910.

And here I had better firmly mark in the family: my father,
John Scott Haldane, whom I sometimes called Uffer, the physiologist and philosopher, a Fellow of New College, but working
mostly in his own laboratory, built onto our house, Cherwell,
at the end of Linton Road in Oxford, with his own team of
young scientists. Behind him Cloan, the family house on the

north-western slope of the Ochills. There lived his mother—
Granniema to me—his brothers, Richard, then War Minister
in the Liberal Government, and Willie, father of the Foswell
cousins, and his sister Elizabeth—Aunt Bay to me. Then there
was my mother, whom I called Maya, with an Edinburgh background, but her mother—Grannie to me—was now a widow
living with us, having brought much of the Edinburgh furniture
down with her. Above all there was my brother Jack in his last
year at Eton and then at New College.

But now let us look for a moment at the process of finding
one's way back in time. Apart from memories, what evidence
have I for what I am going to write? The school diaries which I
used in *Small Talk* came to an end after I left the Dragon School.
There would have been little incentive to write a diary without
competition and the almost certainty of getting a prize! I missed
the school prizegivings, the hall filled with parents who probably
did one credit and one's proud walk up to the platform; the
number of times one managed this in one prizegiving was com-
parable to the number of pink ices one could manage at a party.

But just a diary for its own sake? No. I wrote them occasionally
later in periods of great stress and during the whole of World
War Two, but for the six years from 1910 to 1916 my written
evidence is in letters to, by or about me and occasionally the
Draconian itself, the school magazine, for I still kept up with it
and sent in my poems. It was sad for me now to pass the Dragon
School but no longer to be part of it. So many loyalties were
involved, most of all perhaps to the Skipper, C. C. Lynam.
Clearly he was a marvellous teacher, green-fingered with children,
but dull organisation was not his line. Hum, his brother, was the
organiser and I, instinctively feeling myself on the side of chaos,
was indignant on the Skipper's behalf whenever Hum appeared
to be superseding him and bringing a lot more order into an
ever-growing school, gradually spreading over more and more
North Oxford fields.

For some reason my brother, J. B. S. Haldane, and I were
allowed for a few years to set an annual general paper for the

school. It was full of questions and catches, mostly on modern events or trends (*vers libre*—at that time one never said 'free verse' although I suppose unrhymed verse had really started in America—was translated either as bookworm or 'towards freedom —motto of a political party'). But we ranged through the ages ('Virgil was the mother of Our Lord; there is a picture called the Virgil and Child'). I expect brother Jack must have put in some scientific questions. We marked the papers, wrote a report and enjoyed ourselves. I felt that with this I was still in touch. But how I longed to be once again in one of the Shakespeare plays! How much I wanted the smell of the greasepaint, the lights and the poetry! Sometimes still I dream of this, and great swatches of Shakespeare come back, but I am always afraid of getting my cues wrong.

As for other outside evidence of what we were all like, there are photographs. It isn't always easy to get inside them or remember the occasion, but I know I was taken to be photographed once a year at least. It was the same for Jack. My mother's big desk which had been in the family for two or three generations had a kind of fence of photographs and these also gradually crept all over her walls. It was as though one was forever being pegged down. Yet they quickly ceased to be really me. From the family letters about me it appears that I was admired, encouraged and protected, too much of all three I expect. It gave me a certain kind of over-confidence—so long as I did the right and acceptable thing. Sooner or later if I was ever to be or do anything on my own, this over-confidence had to be reconsidered and broken. But how was one to know?

One thing did break a part of it. I had enjoyed myself very much at the Dragon School. I was for all practical purposes a boy until the awful thing happened. I was twelve, still at the Dragon School, unsuspecting. I had little or no pubic hair; my breasts were ungrown and did not in fact develop until my mid-teens. And then there was blood on my blue serge knickers. I was quickly pulled out of school and I never went back. I couldn't quite understand why, only it seemed that it was something about me which was shameful and must above all never be mentioned to a school friend. It had been a complete surprise, because I had not taken in my mother's carefully veiled and no doubt physiologically inaccurate information. The process was not at all well known at that time, and there were many superstitions about it and little medical help. Even for unbelievers a reading of the Old Testament (those bits of *Leviticus* probably gobbled while one was supposed to be merely taking in the bloodthirsty tribal adventures in *Kings*) with its perpetual reference to uncleanness added to one's unpleasant feelings. For many years I had monthly pain, distress and acute embarrassment; I was taken to various doctors, but, as nobody understood the physiological process, this did not help. The curse, as it was always called, was a main trouble most of my life. After all, it is only in the last twenty years or so that all this has been taken seriously and without embarrassment. In my day men knew nothing or next to nothing about it. Soon after we were married Dick told me that he had been given to understand that ladies had something in the nature of headache every month. Girls of my age were not allowed to swim at these times, which for me sometimes went on for ten days, and were discouraged from many other activities. Tampax did not come in till I was in my thirties, though at least disposables must have arrived with or soon after World War One.

It was all very discouraging and I acquiesced in it, as indeed in other discouragements, but no doubt resentments and determinations built up inside. At a jumble sale I bought a small jug for a penny. It had 'Adventure to the Adventurous' written on it. That, some day, was to be my motto. But meanwhile I went on being what was expected of me. What then, would happen after the end of being a boy at the Dragon School?

If I had been sufficiently determined, I suppose I might have gone away to boarding school, in fact to Priorsfield which, because Mrs Huxley had been headmistress, was acceptable. But two things intervened. My brother would be at New College in a year's time, and I wouldn't want to miss being with him in

Oxford, would I? And did I really want to leave home? Although this was not said in so many words, it was apparent that, if I chose the boarding school, I would hurt the feelings of Those Who Loved One Best. Another solution must be found.

Thus, at twelve I left the Dragon School and found myself with four of those strange beings, girls of my own age. For years in my later life I completely lost touch with all of them; I didn't know if they were alive or dead. They were part of something which had ceased to be real. But in the past, which is the reality about which I write, they are very much alive. Frances, with whom I was friends longest, and whom, only lately, I surprisingly re-found, was grand-daughter of the Warden of Wadham, with two younger sisters, Gwenny and Lily. Shirley too had University parents. Both of these had rather large noses, which would have been no disadvantage with today's fashions and hair-do's, but probably was then, when delicacy of features was more admired. Mary Cooke had this; she was, I think, the niece of J. A. R. Marriott, at one time Conservative candidate for the University, and she had two very pretty, red-haired younger sisters. Her mother was quite a talented painter; she did a romantic water-colour of me, all long fair hair and blue eyes. Finally there was Geraldine, who was plumper, had darker, rather fuzzy hair and lots of freckles. All were definitely young ladies whose brothers or male cousins went to reputable and expensive public schools, where various kinds of learning were shovelled into them, if necessary by the cane, but whose own education was mainly in the hands of a governess with no particular qualifications as a teacher, but possibly the ability to please their mothers, her employers. She stayed with us, in the smallest, north-facing guest room, with her small wardrobe and her few photographs. Her name was Miss Blockey, quickly turned into Blockywox. After we all grew up I went on writing to her occasionally, since by then I had ceased to blame her for my own lack of education; I think in the end she died in some kind of 'home'. I am sure she did her best with five potentially rather bright girls and possibly did less harm than some of the public school masters did to

13

their brothers. But as I came into my teens I was worriedly aware of how far I had slipped behind my old school contemporaries like Jack Slessor, in actual learning of basic school material, though, all the same, I could put no effort into learning on my own.

We had lessons in the school-room at Cherwell, the large new house my parents had built in 1906 at the end of Linton Road, where the hedges had already been cut down and newer houses had been built, in a style slightly more 'rustic' than Cherwell, with lower ceilings and more bay windows with smaller panes, which I thought much nicer than our own big sash windows. The school-room on the top floor was pleasant, with a bit of slope on the ceiling, and plenty of windows to west and north. In the big toy cupboard there were still the boxes of bricks, the rails and rolling stock of the railways that we had played with so often, but suddenly didn't want to. My brother was clearly too old for them; it was no good without him. I never got them out for my classmates; they had to wait for my own children. The old doll's house stood on the landing outside, but again, I hardly ever looked at it now.

Below the school-room was Maya's—my mother's—bedroom, also facing north-west, but the large window mostly blocked by a dressing-table with a full-length mirror and sets of drawers, in one of which were my many hair ribbons; behind was a wicker shoe basket. Here I used to sit in front of the mirror while my hair was brushed and, uncomfortably, combed for scurf, which I felt was somehow shameful and unladylike. Many remedies, suggested by doctors or hairdressers, were tried and had little effect, but some were greasy and meant I had to wear a cap out of doors. These silk caps were quite pretty, but they were not what other girls wore. Naturally, I grew out of scurf in a year or two, so there was really no need to have made me so uncomfortable or ashamed.

Now, Maya's bedroom was one of the least nice of the rooms at Cherwell. The two best, facing south, were for Grannie, her mother, as bedroom and sitting-room, though there was another, smaller and badly proportioned room with windows south and north, which was Maya's own sitting-room or study and where, later, I had a small bureau and bookshelves. When we first moved to Cherwell I had a room of my own, facing over the fields and the river. But after my childhood troubles, a broken leg and after that an operation for a TB neck gland, I had a bed in my mother's room, just under the smaller window; fresh air was thought to be basic for TB. Yet also I am fairly certain that my presence was to ensure that my father should not be allowed in. His room, a rather meagre slice, always smelling of pipe tobacco, was opposite on the other side of the passage, but that side of the marriage was definitely over. She would have been forty-five or so and he some five years older. In her room and in that bed I stayed and dreamed into adolescence.

There was a marble-topped washstand with matching jugs, basins and small ware, above it a medicine cupboard, beyond it a very large dark, carved wardrobe with ample hanging space and deep drawers. The main decoration of my mother's mantelpiece was a large frame of family photographs on a green velvet background—her side of the family. It seemed a crowded room and it is odd, now, to think that she did not move, after Grannie's death, into the big bedroom with the broad south-facing bow, though she did move into the equally pleasant sitting-room. There was a small bedroom between Grannie's bedroom and the bathroom, which had been for Grannie's lady's maid. Perhaps my mother felt that it would be in some way wrong—a deviation from her increasingly spartan way of personal life—to take the nicer bedroom; but at the same time she may have had an undercurrent of resentment at not having a lady's maid of her own.

On the large landing, whose main decoration was a huge gilt-framed pier glass and a marble-topped, gilt-edged sideboard, there was a rather strange WC. It had an outer and inner door. From inside I could hear Grannie shuffling in slow slippers across the landing, opening the outer door and trying the inner, while I stayed very quiet; the brass hook rattled. If she came in? Now, in nightmares, she does. What is the connection? I liked Grannie on the whole and wasn't afraid of her. Was it simply that the shuffle was the approach of old age which I feared desperately? It has come, certainly, and it is very annoying. Why? Villon said it all. But it has brought long experience; it is not simply something that has pounced on me quite unaware between the opening of two doors. In a child's fable I read once, a boy, wanting to be grown-up, unrolls the magic reel and *is*— irrecoverably. I want to go back and forth, as, in a way, I am doing now.

However, there were several other loos in the new house, including the servants' on the back stairs and the 'gentlemen's' through the bicycle-smelling cloakroom off the outer hall, where hats and coats hung. It was down two steps and the only place in the house with a fixed basin—except of course for the lab sinks. It had a red-tiled floor where a drop or two of menstrual blood did not show, as they tended to on the upstairs lino. There was also a faintly forbidden flavour about using it.

But upstairs in the school-room, what did I and the other girls talk about? Plans for games, I suppose, or picnics. Possibly we discussed our parents, swapped stories about them. What, if anything, did we learn? Miss Blockey took us through some history books, asking questions no doubt; nothing remains. History bored me deeply. If she tried to teach English grammar, as she may have done, I was already perfectly capable of handling the language and, usually, the spelling. All of us could write a reasonably good essay. Her own reading was limited and cautious; she was no leader. French progressed slowly. Arithmetic? No doubt it continued. Lately I was asked how one did long division; all I could remember was that one put on two ears. Music lessons went on; there was a piano in the school-room and Miss Blockey played, I suppose, fairly well, and saw to it that I practised scales, easy pieces and singing. The nicest things were the settings of the *Just So* songs. But, apart from College carols, I don't remember ever being taken to a concert or recital.

I doubt if we got anything from any of her other lessons except some smatterings of German; I quite enjoyed reciting bits of Schiller, but *Faust* was proving difficult and perhaps, although a classic, not quite nice. When we were released from the school-room we simply bounded off, running downstairs and out. By this time there was quite a farm at Cherwell, Jersey cows, poultry, pigeons and my own families of guinea pigs. There were the carriage horses and my pony—I suppose nobody ever rode her again after my riding accident—and the pony carriage. There were lots of old hedges—hawthorn and sloe and crab-apple—and it was a good hide-and-seek place.

At first I had been shy of the other girls, never having thought of myself as anything but another boy, but later I got to know them, especially Frances. We went to tea with one another and played versions of the games I had always played, with an element of make-believe, of being someone else, someone more interesting; and we bullied younger sisters and kept them out of our games. Tea in Wadham with Frances was best; we used to have it in a kind of pantry room—or so it was much later in Maurice Bowra's time—from which there was supposed to be a secret passage into Trinity, though we never could find it, even after we moved all the furniture in those back rooms. Afterwards we played in the huge beautiful Fellows' garden, full of great trees, enclosed by mellowed stone walls. I do remember playing prisoners and captives under one of the dark, spreading yew trees and making Frances tie my wrists, though this was perhaps a little later, at fifteen or sixteen. There was a deep excitement about this, not recognisable or at least not nameable at this time. If a grown-up had found us and asked: 'What do you children think you are doing?' we would have collapsed into sullen shame. Sexual shame? Maybe. For me it was all connected with the stories which I still told myself and of which, I suppose, versions persisted into my earlier books and are perhaps recognised by some of the young who are given *The Conquered* to read so as to improve their ancient history. Bedside books, clearly!

But, as for lessons, it must have been apparent that Miss Blockey's amiability and capacity for being put upon concealed serious deficiencies. Perhaps my brother may have pointed this out. I don't know if my father paid any attention to my education or if it was quite outside his world. I went for Latin to Jack Denniston, then a young don. Latin bored me, but I was willing to do a bit of work to please him. I was set for Junior Locals, presumably something in the nature of 'O' Levels, though I am sure on a lower standard in most subjects except perhaps classics; I supposed I would go to university, but with little idea of what this was about; it was just something one did. For a few weeks I was coached in maths by a young woman whose name I have forgotten, but who undid some of the harm of my earlier maths teaching. With her, horizons expanded; I was very happy. One can teach oneself history, geography, some science and some elements of a foreign language, but for maths I think one needs a certain amount of leadership and explanation. I wish I could have gone on, but perhaps that would have been thought silly and extravagant. Later, Jack did some solid geometry with me, which I enjoyed equally.

I missed the excitement and competition of school exams. I had always enjoyed them, especially when they happened, not in the classrooms, but in the school hall. One limbered up for them and then went all out. When, occasionally, I dream about exams, it is usually pleasurable and exciting. So, would this ambitious, competitive young thing have done better at a large school? Would she have been better directed? One thing is clear. Whatever education parents provide for their children, it is always wrong.

II

Rouen to Doncaster

I still had minimal pocket money, sixpence a week perhaps;
I never went shopping on my own, even if it was I who harnessed
the pony and drove the pony carriage down into Oxford. I never
went alone to the Rhea bathing place. When I went out to tea I
was usually taken and fetched, except for the Cookes who only lived
a few houses up Linton Road. Above all I must never be alone in the
Parks, especially not on any of the small paths, nor yet in the
lane beyond the Dragon School, because there might be a Man.
The lane had in large letters on one wall 'Commit No Nuisance';
it was no use asking what this meant but it had something to do
with the Man. I think I was more carefully shepherded now
than when I was at school.

At home I never brushed my own hair and was dissuaded from
trying. I am not sure when I was 'allowed up' for dinner, but even
when this started I was always sent to bed early and obediently
went. Above all, I must tell everything I did and if possible
everything I thought. Yet it would be entirely wrong to say that I
really minded this; it was talking about oneself, always a favourite
occupation, and so long as it was in the right direction, my mother
was tremendously understanding and encouraging. Not being
Truthful, not being Frank with Me, that could be very unpleasant.
I doubt if I was punished, only sadness and disapproval were felt.
But nobody knew what stories I told myself; I was never asked
about them; they were a world.

However, for all this babying, some other quite adult social
activities were encouraged. From my early teens I was one of the
badged Victoria League guides to the parties of overseas visitors,

who came mostly in the Summer Term and who were shepherded round the colleges in groups. I always took mine up New College tower, probably at a brisk trot. The porter always gave me the keys, safer with me than with my father who once inadvertently carried them off to Scotland. I am not at all sure how much actual history of the colleges I knew, but I don't think I was ever at a loss to produce something interesting. At some point in summer there was always a river steamer excursion down to Iffley and beyond; sometimes the Harcourts gave a party in the beautiful garden of Stanton Harcourt, for I remember a tumble of small roses down the terraces and wishing we had anything like that in our flat Cherwell garden with its remarkably unsatisfactory built-up rockery.

This was the pleasantest part of my continuing involvement with Maya's imperialist politics. I did not so much care for the Rhodes scholars, nor for blind 'Trooper Molloy', much used for Empire propaganda and again, at a later stage, for recruiting. There were other young Tory favourites whom I was supposed to look on as extra brothers; no doubt I went along with this after a fashion. I am rather surprised that I never became a Girl Guide; perhaps this would have been in some way unladylike.

In term time there were Sunday tea parties in the hall at Cherwell, with undergraduates, including Rhodes scholars and various cousins who turned up from time to time. The hall had Chinese willow-pattern plates hung on one wall, de Morgan tiles round the fireplace, some splendid bits of furniture and a portrait of Uncle John, Regius Professor of Physiology and first of the family scientists. It also had a grandfather clock whose loud tick sounded through the house at night, apparently chasing one upstairs. There was another in the drawing-room, with a gentler tick, brought south by Grannie with other Edinburgh furnishings. The oldest of the white-aproned removers chided my mother over this: 'Och, Mistress Haldane, what are you thinking on, to put the hall clock in the drawing-room?' But it looked well there.

The drawing-room with the heavy Morris curtains was beautiful. The marble fireplace was carved with laurel wreaths and on the wide shelf were Chinese vases and bowls; the hearth was hand-beaten copper—made, like many of the furnishings, by Charlie ffoulkes, my mother's artistic cousin—and here were the crested fire irons which, unhappily, disappeared at some point; they are somewhat rare. The long bookcase was crowded with china and glass, as was the glass-fronted cupboard above one of the bureaux. Much of this was the very handsome but un-marked Trotter china, probably ordered in quantity by several branches of the family, most likely Worcester. There were also the Lowestoft bowls and jugs, painted in China (many years later we found the crest and directions for painting in Chinese characters) which my mother's grandmother had consigned to the dairy.

The bow-fronted satinwood chest of drawers had the Samoan things which my grandfather had collected when he was consul (being the only English Gentleman—although Scottish—about in those parts at that time) and a few boomerangs which my brother and I got hold of. We were practising with them in the field outside the house when he threw one which decided to come for me. I had seen them dig their sharp points into the ground so decided not to lie down but to hold my own boomerang across my face; the thrown one flickered at me across the space between us; I had time to register what a good war weapon its zigzagging near-invisibility made it; then it hit the one I was holding and slid down it, cutting my finger open. Jack was really upset, but I felt I had been sensible and was pleased with myself.

The other big bureau, made by French prisoners-of-war at Edinburgh Castle during the Napoleonic wars and beautifully inlaid, had much family material, books and documents and the scrap books in red flannel covers. I have it now. It has a secret drawer at the back, but what is exciting enough to put into it? At my age, nothing. But maybe I shall think of something yet.

The drawing-room had a door, always kept locked, into an unsatisfactory little greenhouse, where I tried to grow things. All I was successful with were the cactuses which I stole, as buds or leaves, from the Botanic Gardens and which would suddenly produce astonishing flowers. We never had a gardener who was any good; that would have been an extravagance. Besides, Maya liked to give orders and have them carried out without question, a thing no good gardener could have put up with; she could never have got onto good terms with an Oxfordshire gardener; he would have had to be a Scot, and one never turned up.

I was still a passionately keen wild flower collector. Sometimes the Wild Flower Society, which provided the diaries in which one wrote names and dates, queried my entries, but I would never have cheated over this, whatever else I might have cheated over. I knew all the special wild flower places, the shallow lake and woodland of Ruskin's Plot, Cowley Marsh, now built over, where one used to find some of the rarer orchises; Bessel's Leigh, where I once taught a Sunday School class about Noah's ark; the heights above Hinksey and, further on, the beginnings of the chalk and the rare haunts of *anemone pulsatilla*. Some of these expeditions must have been excessively boring for those who were with me and couldn't possibly have shared my enthusiasm. I suppose it was mostly my mother, and it was the price of keeping an eye on me. There were interesting plants up-river in the edges of water meadow and copse, and then there was Cloan in the summer holidays, with Granniema, my father's mother, who shared my interest and encouraged me to find parsley fern in the screes of Craig Rossie. She was now approaching her nineties and becoming, for me at least, an increasingly genial and interesting figure, with good stories of her young days if one got her to talk about them.

However, we never went back to Cornwall for our lovely, magic holidays at Sennen Cove and I resented this, always asking why couldn't we go. Instead there were Easter holidays in what were supposed to be more educational places. Once we stayed in Dover and went over to Calais on a day trip. But it wasn't like going out with the Sennen boats. Yet one thing stands out; these were the days of early cinema. Jack and I went as often as we possibly could and watched entranced the improbable, captioned adventures of various characters, for these were the days of serials, including the Exploits of Elaine, also of the cinema piano or even orchestra, the pounding of hooves, the chug-chug of the absorbingly oncoming train. As yet the splendid disappearing cinema organ was not with us and many of the cinema halls were somewhat flea-pittish, but if Jack was looking after me it was assumed that all was well.

During Jack's last year at Eton, however, when I was fourteen, it was arranged that in order to improve my French I should stay a fortnight or so with a family at Le Havre, but duly chaperoned by Miss Blockey, and then rejoin Maya and Jack at Rouen en route for Paris. I had one of the Victor Hugo's to read, in fact I was supposed only to read and speak French. Probably I had a Dumas as well. It put me off Dumas and Victor Hugo for life. It seems odd, considering the general censorship, that I should be pushed, at fourteen, into reading *Les Misérables*; however, it was a classic, and in a foreign language. A little later I was also pushed through *War and Peace* in French; it was only when I re-read it, much later and suspiciously, in English, that I realised what sort of book it was. But I was not encouraged to read some of the English classics. *Tom Jones* was strictly kept from me until the time Aldous Huxley came to stay and persuaded my mother that this was Eng. Lit. and an essential part of my education.

However, I ploughed through three or four pages a day at Le Havre. The family also had a couple of young Germans staying— perhaps indeed it was some sort of semi-educational establishment?—and I picked up a little German from them; they always referred to Madame as *die alte Hexe*. I quite liked the harbour area, but mostly we went for walks in the dull suburbs. Perhaps it was more fun for Miss Blockey; she might even have had a mild flirtation.

However, she took me over to Rouen and here an explosive aesthetic experience overtook me. You might think that, living in Oxford, I ought to have been used to Gothic; there is good stained glass in various college windows, including New College. But no. Rouen Cathedral, St Ouen, the clock, the *patisserie*, the thought of Joan of Arc, bound to the stake by soldiers, all combined into a riot of feeling, an alteration of consciousness which I find hard to explain and cannot recover or describe; I only know it happened and that, from time to time in my life, something of the same sort has happened. I drank and drank in the colours of the glass, twined myself into the traceries, quite unable to express any of it, especially to poor old Blockywox who must have wondered what had come over me.

Then we went on to Paris and stayed in a respectable North Bank hotel and ate an excellent *table d'hôte*, but suffered a bit from the current French loos in little corners of the landings. My mother insisted on paper seat covers; I think she always took these about with her, as well as various myths about catching loathsome but anonymous diseases.

Jack and I went to Luna Park and naturally on all the switchbacks and slides and water chutes. At one point we became slightly detached and I was approached by a Man. In fact I think he may have tried to kiss me and I hit him. It was exciting but rather guilt-making, though good for my French. But somehow, if I had behaved as a real lady at all times, it would not have happened, so it was my fault. But why was our mother told? Confession? Or me just wanting to describe something that interested me, a habit I still have but have tried to sublimate in writing books? Or just because we had been brought up to Tell Mother Everything, a very bad principle? Apart from that, we did some shopping at the Bon Marché, ribbons at least.

This business of being a lady was continually besetting me. There were things which, apparently, I should have known by instinct, or if I had listened attentively to what I was told. But I didn't and hadn't. Sometimes I felt as if I was netted by invisible rules, then I would forget. Jack's last year at Eton, when he was nineteen and I was fourteen, seemed to be very full of these invisible rules for a visiting sister. He was by now Captain of the school, multiple prize winner, wielder of a Pop cane. He duly wore a carnation in his buttonhole. For a long time afterwards, the rules of Pop, framed by pale blue-ribboned canes, adorned the school-room. I had of course shared in the general prep school sadism, when one listened outside the headmaster's study for the swish of 'a juicy one'. Normally this went with the bravado of coming out with a swagger but this was not possible for me, although when I had my hair judicially pulled as an equivalent punishment I managed the swagger all right. I think Jack may well have enjoyed an occasional ritual beating, but it was probably going out even in his time, and I doubt if he did it much.

Maya and I went down for the Fourth of June and watched Jack as Lord Burleigh in *The Critics*, though the dramatic performance I still remember was by an earnest young Catholic reciting Heine: *Die Mutter Gottes zu Kevlaar tragt heut' ihr bestes Kleid.* Jack was not one for cricket and my one visit to Lords was only assuaged by many pink ices. He played wall game and was celebrated in verse over this, as well as in one of Ronnie Knox's alphabets with 'H is for Haldane who has a white spot On the back of his head where others have not.' For he had this patch of white hair which occasionally seems to turn up in the family. He was Captain of the Boats too, rowing in the decorated first eight. I longed to swim in the foaming rapids of Boulter's Lock and he had promised to take me, but alas, the curse, coming a few days early, frustrated this. I cried and cried in our hotel room. Clearly there would never be another chance, and I knew, oh yes, I knew, that it would have been as tremendously deep an experience as Rouen.

But the fireworks were fun and the sudden illumination of Windsor Castle. Jack's coevals, who came to gorgeous buttery teas in his study, seemed infinitely witty and interesting. Trev Huxley was one of them, but Julian Huxley, Geoff Wardley and Dick Mitchison, all a year older, had already left. We did an expedition to Burnham Beeches where of course I found a few new plants to look up in the Bentham and Hooker that was always part of the luggage. Eton was still in deep country then, with beautiful walks all round. This Bentham and Hooker obsession has left me permanently with a wish to look things up, to note down plants or birds and when I can't find them I feel faintly undressed. One tangles with the Portuguese of *Flora Zambesiaca* and probably fails to get even the family. But I think I have by now nailed down the immediate flora of Carradale!

Education went on. At home I was in and out of my father's lab a great deal and picked up a little physiology, eked out by reading the small Huxley text book, already, I expect, out of date, and whatever else came my way or was explained by his pupils and colleagues. There were amusing phenomena, including what happened to people's voices after a breath of pure nitrogen. In the inner lab were rows of bottles; one knew about them, more or less. Jack and I administered chloroform to one another, for the delightful sensation of falling among stars. But we sensibly always did this standing up and when we became unable to stand we always stopped.

My father was at this time deeply involved in mine safety and much of his work lay in the central English pits where the main colliery workings were. As a treat I was allowed to go by train to Doncaster to go down Bentley's, one of the deep pits, with him. I knew a certain amount about it, including some of the technical words; I had been shown the capped flame in a miner's safety lamp that spells danger. But actually to go underground was as exciting as Rouen. I wore a black dress, one of those, I am sure, made for me during periods of acute family mourning, I had my own safety lamp. The miners were nice to me, though there was a little teasing during the drop down the deep shaft, where, if one jumped, one shot up. But there was no swearing! They all knew 'the doctor', my father, and respected him for their own virtues: courage and loyalty, hard work and expert knowledge of conditions.

We walked along to the face, saw, smelled, touched, everything. Once I heard singing in the dark distance. I suppose Jack was there too, as I spent the evening with him; we went to the Doncaster music-hall, my first time in such a place, and laughed and laughed. It was totally delightful, a raising of the level of excitement already set off underground among the darknesses and small lights and echoes.

Now, looking back, it seems to me that in the main I only

remember accurately and in any detail the times in my life when there has been this tension of delight, of fear, of pain, of action, when I have been most clearly myself. Yet what is remembered is not the content of the tension, but the facts that aroused it, the people and places, the sounds and smells. Why did some things trigger it off, others not? Psychologists might answer according to different theories. It also means asking oneself about this funny business of memory. What is the process of dredging down, taking off the lids of the memory boxes, recalling smudgily in dreams, sharply through smells? The written word is there, my own letters to Granniema, to Maya, to Aunt Bay, a few to Dick, in upright, legible, ungrown-up handwriting, fluent and full of things observed and set down, mostly natural or personal rather than artefacts, and with a sad amount of clichès about patriotism and all that. There are also my early poems, plays and what-have-you, all too many of which still survive. In these there is an occasional echo of this heightening of feeling, where it breaks through into something written down—and, in a sense, through being put into words, externalised and lost.

III

No Padding on the Bust

I am not quite sure when Grannie died, but it was certainly several years after we moved to Cherwell. I had been old enough to talk with her about books and it was she who introduced me to *The Golden Bough*. She was a great collector of fine lace, and her dresses and caps foamed with it. In looks she was distinctly Jewish, but we never knew of any of the Irish-Jewish relations whom we must have had; there was only the mysterious Miss Joseph, a sudden name in the family tree.

Now she was dead, white and dignified with her silver hair, my first introduction to that mystery. We had to play quietly for a few days and there were comings and goings. We all wore black and arm bands were sewn onto all male jackets. I have no idea where my mother's parents, Grannie and Grandpapa, were buried, presumably in Edinburgh, for I know Maya disappeared for a few days. I only know about my father's mother, Granniema, because, many years later, I was one of the bearers at her funeral and it was somewhat of a state occasion. Later, cremation was normal, though I suppose bits of my brother's body are still around, carefully labelled in Indian academic handwriting. The Oxford Department of Anatomy asked not to have to dissect my father, who had left them his body in his will, as those who would have done it had been his colleagues and pupils. We don't, as a family, hold with material memorials, supposing, with a certain arrogance, that by our works ye shall know us.

In time, Maya moved into Grannie's sitting-room and the old one became full of boxes, files, chairs waiting to be mended and so on. Most of the rooms still had the distemper which, as an economy, had been first put on when the house was built, with the intention of having Morris papers when the walls were thoroughly dried out at a later date which never came. Many years after, I repapered the spare room which I'd lain in during the months of my broken leg, and a few others were done, more or less under protest. We all have our favourite economies.

Much had already silted up in the huge boxroom under the slope of two tile roofs which gradually began to leak; the cross beams constantly knocked our heads as we groped among trunks and screens and mouldering games, plaster busts of the Prince Consort or our own forebears, unliked wedding presents or inheritances, large pictures with broken glass, rolled rugs, things which might come in usefully at some point, and stacks of books, though many that filled the bookcases all over the house might just as well have been stacked—or thrown out. But one didn't throw out in those days. Inexorably things were kept; sometimes they would be just what was needed for a bazaar or jumble sale. However, immediately in front of the boxroom door was the dressing-up box, a very good one with all sorts of gorgeous bits and pieces, hats and parasols and swords. Much had accrued after the deaths of the original owners. (How could a really 'good' piece of material be thrown away?) That didn't worry us. I became more and more addicted to dressing-up games which finally turned into Nebuchadnezzar, that splendid version of charades in which one acted a character who was then one letter of the total word. It was a bit dull being audience, but the grown-ups were always conscripted. I liked being the chief character, Salome or Boadicea or Europa, but we had to have turns.

There was a period of months when all I wanted was to 'go on the stage', which struck me as being perennial dressing-up. The delightful Dowson family lived just round the corner: the twins had been Viola and Olivia in the Dragon School *Twelfth Night*, my last school play, where I was Maria. Their mother, dear Rosina Philippi, had started 'dramatic classes'. We learnt quantities of verse; she taught us how to breathe through rapid declamation; from those days I still know most of *L'Allegro* by heart. But I am sure I was much too self-centred to be a good actor and in time that ambition died, though Frances, who shared it, did go on to act a bit at the Old Vic. For that matter I appeared there once as a troll girl in a raffia skirt for an early production of *Peer Gynt*.

How different dressing-up was from the annual visit of the dressmaker! Before World War One it was most unusual to buy ready-made dresses in shops. Maya paid an occasional visit to her *corsetière* in London and was very distressed when she died and there was no successor. Shops often had dresses in the windows, but if one wanted one it was made to measure, though this was more expensive than making it at home; there were no exact standards of size and almost anything would have to be altered. Once a year, I think, I was allowed a Liberty dress. I had one in a golden rough silk with a square neck cut a little bit low and hand-embroidered in shades of green. With this I wore stagshorn moss in my hair, collected on Craig Rossie, a romantic conception. I think I wore this when I was fifteen or so, perhaps at the dance we had in the house, when all the furniture was taken out of the hall and the floor polished. Miss Williamson, the much-loved waitress who organised all good Oxford parties, arrived to put out the silver and take charge; cakes and jellies and some kind of cup as well as orangeade were laid out in the dining-room. For best I usually had some kind of special thing for my hair, perhaps a spray or circlet of gilt wire, pretty enough and probably ending in the acting box. I had no valuable jewellery but quite a lot of beads, including one very handsome long Chinese necklace of green glass, which Aunt Bay had given me for Christmas in 1912 and which I loved dearly.

But all my ordinary clothes were made by the dressmaker. During the year my mother had bought suitable material for herself and me, especially at the Liberty sales, and put it away in the large chest of drawers in the spare room that faced west and in which the dressmaker would install herself and her machine, probably sleeping in the small room next door. I had little choice, though the brighter colours were for me, and often trimming was supplied by bits and pieces from foreign parts, especially Chinese or Indian embroidery. I am sure I had a white dress of Madras embroidered muslin. Unbleached linen and tussore silk were both well thought-of materials, in some way more connected with the world of good intentions. My mother's dresses almost always had lace for edgings, and this was carefully unpicked when a dress was to be discarded. I sometimes had a piece of Bucks or Valenciennes for a collar, but it was thought that I was still too rough for good lace. It was borne in on me that no lady ever wore anything but 'real' lace. Or real pearls.

I suppose I could have turned down anything I really hated, but clothes were not that important, just something that had to happen to one. I don't remember anything in the nature of a fashion book, still less being at all pleased at the prospect of being fitted, the endless measurements, with one's skirt coming nearer the ground every year, and always the long, slow turn round while the hem was pinned and measured and the fusty smell of the dressmaker herself. A drugget was put down on the floor so that the pins shouldn't escape. An uneven hem would have been really immoral. One wore a petticoat-bodice and petticoat on the top of woollen, or in summer cotton, combinations and knickers buttoned below the knee, but even so, dresses were carefully scanned in case it was possible to 'see through'.

There was an attempt, when I was around sixteen, to put me into a laced corset, an unattractive contraption of heavy white cotton, whale-boned. But I firmly said it stopped me breathing when the waistline was pulled in, so that was given up and the whole thing came down round my knees. I think Maya was a bit half-hearted about it. The waspies of the early forties shocked me, even though they were never as tight as their predecessors; it wasn't a fashion that lasted long.

I was supposed to wear a hat out of doors almost always. They were mostly plain felts or straws, except for those wretched silk caps, but one could choose a ribbon for one's boater, or have a piece of one's dress material hemmed. In winter one wore woolly caps of some kind. Again, I don't remember fashion pictures, at any rate not in our house. I would never, somehow, have thought of fashions as applying to me and I don't think my classmates talked about them.

What seems in some way oddest about this is that instead of thinking what was prettiest or would suit one best, the essential was to wear the right clothes for one's station in life. The curious word 'suitable' was one which was often employed: 'dainty', 'graceful', 'elegant' and so on were for upper-class clothes, 'useful' for the lower orders, though I think 'hardwearing' would be employed for men's tweeds at all levels. Clothes accentuated class divisions and of course one was uncomfortable if one dressed out of fashion, unless that is one had deliberately broken with the range of class custom. I did that later on as a young married woman, though I was still following a fashion of some kind: the Isadora Duncan fashion, or later the Augustus John fashion, low-waisted linen in strong colours which I liked very much. But in my teens it would have been impossible. It wasn't that one wanted to wear the right clothes but one somehow ended in feeling uncomfortable if one didn't. It was too bad if fashion did not favour one's figure or colouring, but there was little one could do about it.

Today I find myself worried by the return of long skirts and the eagerness of young lovelies to hop into them. I have to remind myself that they can equally easily hop out. We couldn't, and so we fought against them, gaining a few inches of ankle revealment after 1914 when it became clear that more and more things could be done by women if once their clothes could be rationalised. I am put off Laura Ashley by the subconscious realisation that so many of her materials and dresses, including the general buttoned-up look and high necks, would have been thought highly suitable by my mother.

One nice dress, which I enjoyed, was when I was bridesmaid to Peggy Lane Poole, green with some deep pink embroidery somewhere on the bodice, a crinkly, ankle-length silk. I am sure Peggy talked my mother into a mild extravagance and I know it was suggested that the dress might have a little padding on the bust.

Maya turned this down and I felt rather insulted, both by needing to have it and then by not being allowed to. The wedding was great fun, though; we all knew one another well and there were ices. Weddings among family and friends usually meant choosing a present, a small piece of silver; we went to one of the antique shops and usually found something nice and not too dear; gradually I formed a degree of good taste in such matters and even an awareness of price.

There was one dress which I remember even better. It was for Henley, my first—and only—time there. How it started was that there was a girl called Charlotte Allen whom I loved and thought beautiful and admirable, and I was to have a dress the same as hers. It was white ribbed silk with a black velvet sash; we had black wired muslin picture hats with cherries on them; perhaps the colour repeated on the sash. But at Henley it rained and the red on the punt cushions came out and stained my white dress like blood. And then Charlotte got appendicitis and her parents were Christian Scientists, so she died, in considerable pain one would suppose, and that was the end of that. I cannot even now pass the gate to that house without a return of misery.

In my early teens there were a certain amount of children's parties, not so nannied as earlier ones in Edinburgh, but still we were under general supervision. We played party games and sometimes danced, usually things like Sir Roger, Swedish Dance and Lancers. There might even be pink and blue programmes with pencils attached by fluffy silk ties, and one knew that a lady didn't have more than two or perhaps three dances with the same partner. I went to dancing classes at the High School, in a long room with windows facing Banbury Road. I was clumsy and heavy-footed and none of the dances came naturally to me. There were free exercises to a tinkly piano, but it would have taken more than these to make me graceful. The classes seemed stupid anyhow, part of this lady thing. At parties I was quite confident most of the time, but every now and then I realised that I was too fat, a podgy little girl, that I wasn't growing any taller, and had no bosom, or at least none compared with some of my friends. I remember one such party where I crept away and up the stairs and on the top landing found a splendid rocking-horse; on it I rode, happily telling myself stories, while the dance music and the laughing went on below.

There was however one wonderful party at Sir Arthur Evans's house on Boar's Hill. He did not, I think, ever ask young ladies who had come out, preferring the genuine *parthenos*. It was the best party I had ever been at, a cotillion with favours and lots of grown-up dancing and Japanese lanterns. But in glass cases here and there were the things from Knossos, the gold and the bulls, and I dragged my partners over to see them, and the same excitement, the tension and delight, caught me again.

I don't remember what I wore at any of these parties; probably I didn't even choose it, but was told what to wear and had it buttoned for me if the buttons were behind. I had little chance of developing any taste of my own. My sixpence a week was of course worth a lot more than it would be today—there were plenty of penny commodities—but I had no regular allowance at all until I was about to be married, so that I had no notion of spending sensibly. I never went shopping; I was taken shopping. There is a big difference.

There were few babies in my young life and I avoided them. I thought younger children were on the whole silly and a nuisance. Young babies had nannies and they dribbled and smelled. I think my mother was worried about this distaste of mine. She took me once to see a friend's baby being washed and dressed. Clearly she thought this baby was very nice. I did not find it so.

IV

Books and Plays

All these years I read and read. At one point much to my annoyance I had to wear steel-rimmed reading glasses. Either they caught in my hair or they were uncomfortable round my ears. Ever since the operation on my neck gland I had an over-sensitive feeling about my neck close to the ears, an erogenous zone the other way round.

My reading was very mixed. After the Dragon School I remember no school books, only the choking dullness of any history people tried to turn me onto. I was still reading a fair number of children's books, including *Jock of the Bushveld* (predictably, several times, the scene of the beating of the Zulu) and with occasional lapses into the really sentimental. But also I was devouring Kipling and by now the science fiction Wells, and perhaps *Mr Polly*. There were bits of sociological or political slanting which I am sure had far more effect than the same thing presented straight, which I would probably not have read. In a way *Kim* had as much influence as any, not so much the imperialist, super-snob message which I accepted as a matter of course, but the idea of non-attachment, loosing oneself from the Wheel. I began to look at the amount of things that filled Cherwell. Things. Some intrinsically beautiful or valuable. Others just being there. Being things. Objects of attachment.

Now, I had a collection of little celluloid men with weighted bases so that they sprang upright. They lived on the top of my bureau; they were in different designs, a Chinaman, a Red Indian, a Scottie and so forth, bright colours, and I was constantly playing with them, almost talking to them. They pulled me back, attaching me to the Wheel. There was some kind of request for some charity or good cause. I swept them off into a cardboard box and gave them away, with pain of course, like a Creator deciding that He (She?) mustn't get too much attached to these little, silly men and women and burying them all under a tidal wave. Once, some years later, I found myself getting too much attached to a piece of modern pottery—a nice one, I think—and broke it. This probably helped me to travel light or, if I had attachments, to have them in terms of use or even as charms against danger or bad luck, which I knew to be completely ineffective, except that they fulfilled an admittedly irrational need. There was the *sgian dubh* given me by the people of Carradale which I took to London during World War Two and which helped me through air raids, in the sense that I was less frightened and because of that behaved better, more sensibly and with more regard for others. Many people used such charms, entirely realising that this was all they were. Dick, for instance, felt much safer in an air raid if he had his umbrella.

Yet perhaps the most important Kipling influence was simply style. The straight descriptions in *Kim, Rewards and Fairies*, and many other Kipling novels and stories, are written with superb clarity and colour. My own early writing is closely and even embarrassingly modelled on Kipling; one could do worse. D. H. Lawrence, splendid in some ways, was unfortunate as an early influence on some writers. No writer can immediately start with a developed, individual style.

I was at the same time reading a fair amount of rubbish. I don't count Wodehouse as rubbish, though I am not sure how well his school stories would survive. But how I looked forward to *The Captain* and the doings of Psmith every month! It was the only children's magazine we ever had in the house. Not for me *Chums* or *Beano*. A little later, at seventeen or so, I had a crush on Zane Grey, but I read *The Virginian* earlier, and Gene Stratton Porter, though I can't now remember the name of one of her books. There were baddish historical novels, Bulwer Lytton's *Last Days of Pompeii*, and Whyte Melville's *The Gladiators*, with which I was much obsessed, but not Scott, because, no doubt, I'd had him for school compulsory reading. I was much moved by a series of novels about the American Civil War, always from the side of the Old South. With all these books, and indeed with others, I tended to continue the conversations, at least those which were full of emotion, beyond the point where the author (doubtless on purpose and wisely) had stopped them. I encouraged all the pent-up passions to run out through me in 'day-dreams'. Occasionally I still do this even with my own writing, but am well aware of the kind of thing it is.

However, the popular, but actually rather bad writers had no stylistic effect on me. A writer who had more was R. L. Stevenson, in spite of *Treasure Island* and *Kidnapped* being school reading. Yet the fact that *Kidnapped* had been something one got marks on in an exam stopped me from re-reading or continuing to *Catriona* until decades later. What I liked were *The Wrong Box*, *Island Nights' Entertainments* and the *Fables*. The beautiful big edition was in the library at Cloan, lovely to read in. I made some efforts to read what was supposed to be superior fiction, partly because Jack wanted me to read whatever he specially liked. But I stuck in Conrad, Meredith and Henry James, though now I much enjoy Conrad, and am not ashamed to say how boring I find the other two. In my late teens I stuck in Dostoevsky who, later on, in my fifties, I found so fascinating. Dickens, of course, was still hopelessly a holiday task. At around sixteen I discovered Hugh Walpole and read all his books with passionate absorption, though now I can remember nothing of any of them.

Censorship continued spasmodically. I wasn't allowed to read *The New Machiavelli*, and when I peeped into it and found it wasn't science fiction, I didn't really want to. Among our ancestral books I was forbidden *The History of Highwaymen*, as well as *Tom Jones*.

There was a collected Poe at Cloan, small volumes appropriately bound in crimson cloth. I don't think it would affect me now, but then I read *The Pit and the Pendulum*, *The Masque of the Red Death* and all the rest with continuous shock and fascination. The raven Nevermore was as serious for me as it was for Gauguin. Did this climate of romantic horror vanish for ever with our own genuine horrors hitting us from every page of every newspaper? Or has science fiction taken over? But that should not be romantic.

Poe's horrors were all the worse at Cloan, since they were so close akin to those which I half expected round every turn of the spiral stair or waiting in the curtains of the four-posters. I was tautened up ready for them. At this time, too, I unwisely read James's *Ghost Stories of an Antiquary*. There would have been a case for censoring this, at least to me. I read other, lesser ghost stories, including *The Hound of the Baskervilles*, and was frightened, but James got me where it really hurt. I still dislike sleeping in a room with a second bed in case this follows the story of *Oh Whistle and I'll Come to You*. I have never written a ghost story, though I expect, out of various experiences, I could write a fairly unpleasant one. But why deliberately and for no good purpose add to the world's fears and unpleasantness?

These were much further away in those days; one only heard of terrible wars and earthquakes and fires long after the agony was past. I hardly ever read *The Times*, which of course was our newspaper, except that in Scotland there was also the *Scotsman*. I had little idea of what was going on in the world; it was not near or immediate. However, for Scots upper-class gossip, my mother depended on Aunt Christian—Mrs Fraser Tytler, born Kerr. They not only wrote to one another, lengthily and often, but tended to be so much *en rapport* that they knew when something was happening to the other. This was my mother's only concession to non-rationality, though the servants were quite encouraged to go to church.

Yet my main enthusiasm was always poetry. I read the Victorians, lots of Tennyson and Browning, though I missed out some of the longer verse dramas, Rossetti and a number of minor authors and finally Swinburne—almost all Swinburne except the very late poems. Why wasn't Swinburne censored? Well, poetry never was. Being poetry made it all right. I knew masses by heart and declaimed it, either aloud or to myself: *Dolores, Atalanta,* the lot. One of my favourite things was to get Miss Blockcy to play the piano while I danced and declaimed. What did she play? I suspect old-fashioned waltzes to which timing much of Swinburne goes admirably. Clearly I wasn't going to act on the maxims of Dolores. Anyhow Swinburne was dead and therefore a classic. Sometimes Frances and I danced together, doing what we supposed were very daring mimes: 'The lovers whose lips would excite thee, Are serpents in hell.' How serpentinely we writhed!

But I read very little Shelley, though now I enjoy him, especially the science fiction aspect of *Prometheus Unbound.* I couldn't be doing with Wordsworth, nor yet Milton, although Jack admired him so much. I liked Coleridge, but my reading did not go much earlier, except for the ballads. My last prize from school and the only one that is still with me, was the *Oxford Book of Ballads.* I swam around in these and was not even averse to Scott's pastiche ballads, though I found his long poems boring. I think that what I looked for in poetry was magic, the light through Rouen Cathedral windows, the dead drop of the mine shaft: '*It fell about the Martinmas when nights are lang and mirk*'. Lyrics and ballads provided this fuel. I now ask myself, was I looking for the equivalent of a drug experience in altered consciousness? If so, would some of our present teenage addicts find that poetry isn't bad for getting high on? But to do this it probably has to have a very definite rhythm and evocative force. Also, I think it must be straight. So much modern poetry is ironic or deliberately held on a low note; that may be artistically admirable, but it doesn't send the reader.

In my mid-teens I got into the habit of turning over the newest poetry books at Blackwell's to see what there was. They were very amiable about letting one do this in the old days. I had at one time been puzzled by the Latin concept of the strict metrical foot and only later began to understand about stress. Once or twice I was taken up to the Poet Laureate's house on Boar's Hill; I was somewhat in awe of Bridges himself, but I think he must have dropped a sentence or two on verse construction, which was helpful. It must have been he who told me to read Hopkins, but I didn't until later. It is most improbable that there was a Hopkins among the poetry books in our house.

Although I was so put off by the set school books if they were novels, I had never minded learning poetry by heart. I knew a great deal of Shakespeare, but also *Lays of Ancient Rome*, *The Armada* and so on. Sometimes at school we were told to do illustrations; I always had glorious ones in my head, great allegorical figures, towers and flags, but my niggling pencil and scrawling chalks always betrayed me. Sometimes later on I tried to draw on my own, but it was no good. I expect I would have been happy to produce something like Bernard Partridge's drawings in *Punch*. We took *Punch* and I always opened it hoping to find one of Bernard Partridge's noble Britannias in the act of protecting a minority or, in justified imperial anger, punishing an offender. We also had quantities of bound back volumes from some of which I learned a bit of nineteenth-century history. These were in the revolving bookcase in the dining-room and I used to take them out and read them sitting on the end of the sofa, or even behind it, in a way which irritated any grown-up and induced them to send me off to do something useful. One of the other large sets of books in this bookcase was the complete Jowett translation of Plato; in the process of twirling the book-case, the contents of which sometimes cascaded onto the floor, I picked up and began to read *The Republic* and was much taken with the idea of being a Guardian. This, I know, started off one of my interminable inside stories, interspersed with noble sayings in the manner of Jowett.

It is odd that I was not put off by the undoubted fact that all Plato's Guardians were male and that he said many unpleasant things about the inferiority of women. But in my inside stories I don't suppose I was ever a Greek woman. I am sure, however, that in common with only too many upper-class British, I got a lot of curious ideas from Plato. Some fitted in excellently with my mother's view of politics and the superiority of the State (in her case the Empire) over any individual, who must always be ready to sacrifice his or her self, or be sacrificed, for the Greater Good. In World War One, parents 'gave' their sons.

Now it remains that there is a human need for something, if need be, to die for. Without it, life is less interesting. But why the State? The rot spread even to the Christian martyrs whom I rather enjoyed reading about; their State was the heavenly city. And again, Plato was always full of chat about leadership. Yes, from time to time my stories enthroned me as a philosopher-king. But what did it all lead to in the twentieth century? The *Fuhrerprinzip*, the totalitarian state and the English public school. But this was something I was not to see for a long time. Perhaps I only escaped the Platonic net, so widely spread in Oxford, by being one of those inferior creatures of the wrong sex, born, not to be leaders, but perhaps with luck, like Socrates (not to be confused with his caricature in *The Republic*) to be a gadfly.

There was a curious convergence of views on the State between my mother and her disapproved-of brother-in-law, Uncle Richard, when he produced the theory of *sittlichkeit*, which she couldn't help agreeing with. To be a good citizen in the sense of active accord with the noblest ideals of one's State or loyalty-group (for instance, the British Empire) might have been the thought behind it, in reaction against the largely selfish individualist motives of the 'shopkeeper'. But when the State itself goes bad? Somehow that thought had been kept under. Thus *sittlichkeit*, product, via Hegel, of Plato, turned out to be a short, though as yet not obvious, step towards the theory of the Master Race, alone truly *sittlich*. Later on, Smuts's holism, a further stateward development, leading to the present South African situation, attracted them both. Smuts was, of course, a charmer; he quickly conned my mother into forgetting he was a Boer.

So there I was, sitting on the dining-room floor, probably twirling the bookcase with one hand and absorbing Plato. In another corner of my stocking-up was Ayton's *Lays of the Scottish Cavaliers*, illustrated. This too had a mystique which, in modern phraseology, sent me. But, oddly enough, it never led me to find out exactly what Montrose had been doing or why Argyll was the master fiend: that would have been history and *ipso facto* dull.

One day in the drawing-room Jack came in with a small red book and in a state of great excitement. It was the first Housman. He stood beside the satin-wood inlaid occasional table, which had a small book trough on it with tiny books, mostly dark brown leather from the eighteenth century, edifying works of some kind, un-read. There was a silver-handled tortoiseshell paper knife and a few other bits and pieces, probably a vase of flowers; it was usually I who did the drawing-room flowers. He began to read aloud from the small red book. Later I seized on it too and in no time we had half the poems by heart. For a while no other poet, not even Swinburne, counted or measured up to *The Shropshire Lad*.

It was Jack, also, who put me onto reading Shaw. Reading plays was fun, though not as good as acting them, but seeing them was the next best. We went regularly to the Oxford theatre; the seats were not very expensive, though we usually had stalls. I can still see the curtain with its vaguely Renaissance house party enjoying a little music. How one's eyes fixed on it for the first tremble before it went up! We all liked to be there in good time, and were very cross if other people came in late.

I suppose my first sight of the theatre was a Christmas pantomime. I have an idea it was *Jack and the Beanstalk*, with a splendid interior curtain of beans for the principal boy, Jack, to climb. This was the 'transformation scene', a bit of formal magic always included and something specially to look forward to. I think, too, that these early pantos ended with a harlequinade, with strings of sausages coming out of the clown's baggy white pants, but a little frightening because of the red-hot poker. And I have another faintly uneasy feeling about my first experience of the theatre. Can it be that I wetted my drawers?

From about twelve I was taken fairly regularly to Shakespeare, usually the Benson company. I remember *Coriolanus* best and how much I sympathised with him. There was not much artifice about these productions, but it was straight Shakespeare with the

42

big speeches properly hammed, as I would like to have done myself. One could gloat over the words, not being distracted by clever production. In the classical dramas, everyone wore white sheets, possibly decorated with a key pattern, or purple for Caesar. For a long time I thought of the Romans and Greeks as marblish, sheeted figures of this kind, until in fact I began to write about them and had really to think what they looked like.

All the family enjoyed the theatre, but especially my father; he had few other recreations, except for croquet which he played with maddening exactitude, lying down on the grass and sighting the balls, jumping with frustration if he failed to bring off a shot. It is he whom I remember taking me, in my early teens, to Galsworthy and an occasional Shaw. Those were the days when one really listened to the dialogue! Scenery was strictly realistic, clothes much what one knew elsewhere, unless it was a historical play, in which case, again, there would be nothing unexpected nor offensive to the good taste of North Oxford. But how exciting the Galsworthy 'problem plays' were! *Justice, Strife, The Silver Box*—one followed every word. There tended to be a bit of family argument over Shaw as some plays were thought unsuitable for me. These I usually contrived to read. And, as I was always writing plays myself, it was essential that I should see as many of them as possible. I managed on the whole to convince people of this.

Gilbert and Sullivan came once a year and there was always a tremendous University rush for tickets. I always longed to go as often as possible, but the D'Oyly Carte Company was not considered as educative and edifying as Galsworthy. For some reason it was thought that *The Yeomen of the Guard* was more suitable than *Pirates* or *Mikado*, but I remember *Iolanthe*, and vaguely wondering if Uncle Richard had ever had to deal with a beautiful ward in chancery when he was Lord Chancellor. Some of my friends used to stand in the gallery queue, but I was never allowed.

But around the time I was fifteen or sixteen we had the Abbey Theatre group with Synge, Yeats and Lady Gregory. There was a superb performance of *The Playboy of the Western World* which seemed in quite a different class from anything I had ever seen. It wasn't acting; it was being. I find it difficult to remember which of the others I actually saw performed, since, in reading them, I visualised the stage so clearly. Did I see *Countess Kathleen*? I don't know. With Shaw one has such definite stage directions that it is impossible not to visualise, but it is a little surprising that I did it with all plays.

When I was fifteen or so, my brother and I started going up to London occasionally to see plays, or perhaps the cinema, but I don't think we took that seriously; it was just an amusement. With luck we got in a matinée and an evening performance. Once we were taken out to lunch at Brown's Hotel—lobsters—by Mavro, my father's young colleague, the one who was nicest to us. Once we ate a very nasty vegetarian meal at the Eustace Miles restaurant, appropriately after Shaw. That evening we went to a variety show at the Coliseum with two unforgettable things: Sarah Bernhardt, then an old woman, as Theodora—in French and the first time I realised the point of understanding it—and a Russian dancer. Could it have been Pavlova? Oh, that was magic, that was delight, staying with us all through the journey back in the midnight train from Paddington!

The plays I wrote when I was still at school never got as far as the stage, but the one I wrote at fifteen did. The dear Skipper, whose pet I always was, let us do the play during the holidays in the hall of the Dragon School on the stage where our Shakespeare plays had been performed, and the whole thing was published as a supplement to the *Draconian*. Possibly I was the first O.D. to have a play performed; it was certainly my first experience of correcting proofs.

The play was about an imaginary country, Saunes Bairos, in the Andes under a vaguely Mayan culture, about which I had picked up such items as suited me, for instance the use of quipus for messages. In the play the population was firmly kept down by a hierarchy of priests and the plot involved the birth of twins (one too many) to an important personage in the state. There was a prologue featuring two modern geneticists and several guinea pigs and then the main play with my brother as Cahu Halpa, the father. His opening lines, 'Twins, my god, twins!' was said to have lifted out of their seats and out of the hall one or two of the more respectable members of the North Oxford community. The valley of Saunes Bairos was guarded at the snow-line, and nobody until the coming of the perfect race, was let through, either way, I suppose, but at the climax of the play the girl twin (who but me?) leads a courageous band of followers, one of whom (who but Jack's friend Dick Mitchison?) watches with her the new dawn, across the snow-line to a rather uncertainly imagined freedom from the priests.

Re-reading the play, it is juvenile, but not as juvenile as all that. There is a sense of theatre, tension, and lively or occasionally poetic writing, with some charming songs, though the Kipling influence is rather too strong. But there are some curious bits in the modern prologue and epilogue, where the two geneticists are talking eugenics: '. . . things like the Mental Deficiency Bill, which is supposed to be charitable and really succeeds in being grossly unjust to the poor'—an echo from my brother perhaps? And again: 'Think what it would be for us if one merely had a rule for eugenics within the Empire! It would do more than preference or even federation.' Echoes of my mother clearly. Yes, I liked to please, and also to show how bright I was.

There was an enormous cast, largely Jack's Eton and Oxford friends and of course my class-mates—even Miss Blockey was roped in. I seem to remember writing in small parts for those who would have been 'hurt' not to be in. They are all in the large photograph taken in the corner of New College cloisters and it was 1913. There is Hartley the chief priest, whose dark and regular features fluttered my heart, killed two years later, and Gerald Boswell the snow-guard who sang my song: '. . . and all the land lies far below, Below the snow-line and the snow, The snow-line changing never,' walking up and down with his spear, making up the tune which I remember as lovely: killed too. Moss Blundell who drew brilliant cartoons of us all: killed in the same year.

45

War and death, suddenly coming real, hit us, only sparing half-blind Aldous Huxley, the 'old priest'.

All this meant a lot of gorgeous dressing-up, and I busily made quipus out of coloured wool. I don't remember what I wore except that it included the green Chinese necklace. I do remember with some shame being dreadfully fussy about the words and jumping on those who didn't say them right. There was also a Canadian friend, David Hossie, who got through the war without even a wound, recovered from the 1918 'flu and became a successful lawyer: he pronounced lamas—part of my local colour—with a short American 'a' which convulsed us all. I can't think how we had time for all this, but no doubt the absence of domestic chores did make a lot of time available and nobody was in quite such a hurry to cram in everything. Time's winged chariot wasn't such a hoverer, and Oxford undergraduates didn't work so hard. A nice well paid professional job would no doubt turn up for all of them in good time.

It seemed to me that acting a play at least once a year was an essential part of life. I was much taken with Maurice Hewlett's *Pan and the Young Shepherd*. But there were passages in it which my mother found 'unsuitable'. I am not at all sure what her criterion was, but she made me cut or re-write them and then send the result to Maurice Hewlett, who very properly turned down the proposal to act his mangled play with a loud bang. How did I allow myself to get into this position? I know I was uncomfortable about it, but there was this business of no lady being able to speak the banned lines, all incredibly mild. It was part of a whole stifling climate and I acquiesced. There was one terrible blame-word: *suggestive*. I remember watching the male guinea pigs agitating around the females with their very typical chittering (and these were important matings from the standpoint of experimental genetics) and quoting, 'In the Spring a young man's fancy Lightly turns to thoughts of love.' I was heavily jumped on for saying something suggestive and felt deeply ashamed for weeks.

The year when I was sixteen we did a double drama in the warm, unclouded July of 1914, using the tennis court as auditorium and acting on the slope above it. One of these was mine, *Prisoners of War*, a drama about Roman prisoners of a Sarmatian king who recognises a fellow Mithraist: something of a crib from Kipling. Jack was the Sarmatian king, Dick the Mithraist prisoner, Gervas Huxley the chief priest (I seem to have had a thing about chief priests). I, of course, was the king's daughter in a yellow dress with my hair hanging all over it and someone's fur stole on one shoulder. My brother wore an enormous wolf (goat?) skin rug. I wrote a poem about him, not very good. The Mithraic sacrament was taken in a two-handled copper pot, which I gave Dick afterwards, inscribed: *Militi Mithrae filia regis Sarmaticae d.d.* But it wasn't much good for flowers as it started leaking and it went in the fire at Carradale in 1969.

The other play was Gilbert Murray's translation of *The Frogs*. Here the chorus, led by me on one side and Frances on the other, moved round a turf altar, wreathed with yellow tree lupins, while the main drama went on at a higher level. We made a lot of minor alterations on the spot: 'Lethe, North Oxford and the rest of hell.' And we turned the little oil-can into an umbrella; I'm sure Aristophanes would have been delighted. It was all marvellous fun, waking up to another summer day of creative excitement and activity, escape into delight, though there were still those awful times when one's period was on, and one felt something might shamefully show and one wondered if one smelt, and people would get to know. Sex raising its ugly head and *hurting*. Meanwhile my mother was beginning to worry about Ulster. Needless to say she was a passionate loyalist and Carsonite: 'Ulster will fight and Ulster will be right.' I began to foresee conflict with my Liberal father, which I didn't want because I was just beginning to see another political side to things, but I needn't have worried. Something else was coming to distract Tweedledum and Tweedledee: the monstrous crow blackening the skies of Europe.

Lewis Gielgud, another old Etonian, elder brother of John and Val, came into my life then, to stay there till his death. He was Dionysos in *The Frogs* with Gervas Huxley as Xanthias, his slave,

47

with his long legs touching the ground at each side of the small donkey; but Lewis also stage-managed my play and the choruses of *The Frogs*. He was almost professional, the real stage in his blood and we fought like cats and yelled at one another; he wanted to alter my sacred words—and I would now suppose that he was perfectly right. Also he told me that I didn't scream convincingly and again I am sure he was right; I probably squeaked. He brought his sixteen-year-old brother John into my next play, *Barley, Honey and Wine*, the last of my lost adolescence, post-war. Much later, in Paris, we wrote play after play together, modern or historical, only one of which ever got acted, and only in a very small way. They were competent, professional plays and we were always very hopeful about them, but we never managed to hit the fashion: our hue was not the wear. Only we laughed and worked and laughed as I never laughed again afterwards. So perhaps it was worth while.

Captain of the School, Eton, 1910. Jack and me

Saunes Bairos. A drawing by Aldous, 1913. He sits, as the old priest, behind Hartley

V

Change

A good many changes took place between 1909 and 1914, but how aware were we? Not very. Certainly we looked at the sky. Once, when I was still a school child, a balloon floated over Oxford. I ran full pelt down Bardwell Road to tell them at school—for some reason I wasn't there at the time. It seemed an adequate excuse for everyone, masters and boys, to rush out and wave madly while the beautiful shining object wavered past. A few years later, and it was an early biplane giving a show in Port Meadow. Jack and I hurried there to watch it hedge-hopping hugely and impressively, faster surely than a train or a motor-car, the fastest things we knew. The crowd ran to look; we heard it roaring and then it was coming straight at us, or seemed to be, over the tops of the hawthorns. But neither of us could foresee ourselves casually getting into a flying machine. The first domestic planes I flew in were certainly biplanes on the smaller Highland runs, nice, friendly little things.

By 1914 London had motor-buses but they had open tops which were great fun if one could induce whatever adult one was with to climb. There were still some trams, including the splendid one that plunged underground from the Embankment to Kingsway, and in Edinburgh and Glasgow the trams were the order of the day for public transport. We still went first class on the underground, the Circle mostly, though we almost always went second on a real train. Sometimes Jack and I went third and it seemed very daring and even dangerous.

The deep freeze and even the household fridge were far in the future, so fruit and vegetables were seasonal and all the more looked forward to and enjoyed. There would be gluts of home-grown fruit, strawberries, plums, pears and so on; the green-grocers' bushel baskets were full and buzzing with flies. Prices dropped and everyone turned to and made their own jam. Tinned produce was not very good and we were always on the look-out for blown tins and the new ptomaine poisoning. I don't suppose my mother ever had any tinned meat product in the house. Cold meat was carefully put under fly-proof covers in a north-facing larder.

We had a telephone installed—the kind where one turned a handle—in the passage at the back of the dining-room, no peaceful corner for long conversations. But it certainly had not taken the place of letters; it was there mainly for my father's dealings with Government departments, or for ordering from shops. One wasn't getting its full use.

In those days games and sports were still amateur, largely happening at universities and the larger schools. Maybe there were rough games like soccer in the north, but no attention was paid to them. The immense market for sports goods had hardly begun, though a good cricket bat was thought to be an acceptable present for any boy. Winter sport was still skating, curling in Scotland, sliding, snowballing or tobogganing on tea trays. There were splendid runs at Cloan, down from the terrace walk almost into the burn. One was apt to get a bit of a bang at the bottom on some of the rocks; but that was part of the fun. As for me, I swam when-ever I could, though we did not go regularly to the sea; once we went to North Devon, but I still felt that Devon was subtly inferior to Cornwall and when I got up to my knees in a quicksand I was sure of it. Sometimes in summer I deliberately tangled with other boats on the Cherwell, in the hope that my own canoe would upset, as it occasionally did. If it had some young man in it who hoped to rescue me, that made it all the funnier, as I was usually a better swimmer even with my longish skirt and Sunday hat. I was a fairly expert paddler, Canadian style, and used to go quite a long way up, sometimes telling myself exploration stories.

The lower part of the river was getting crowded. By 1914

Timms' boat-hiring was in full swing. But we now had our own boathouse, a pleasant little building roofed with Stonesfield slates. Here we had a rowing boat, for my father still enjoyed rowing for a few years longer, a punt and two canoes, one of which I had saved up for over several years; she was called *The Ship of Fools*. There were rollers for the boats to go down and a ricketty wooden ladder off the landing-stage into the greeny-brown water, and there I swam in my so-enclosing serge bathing dress, with a towel over my shoulders afterwards in case I showed my figure.

There were water weeds then, which gently stroked one's legs in the mild current, but in winter there were always floods. These brought fertilising mud down onto the water meadows, still marked with low ridges from earlier strip cultivation, from which one could always get two hay crops year after year. I suppose the floods are now controlled and much less interesting, and perhaps there are fewer marsh flowers. I always helped with the hay, of which we had a big, square stack.

For there was also my mother's farm. The Jersey cows were heavy milkers; it was of course all hand-milking and there was no cooling of an acceptable modern kind. The milk cans were put into the shade and, for the house, poured into white enamel setting pans in the slate-shelved, north-facing small dairy. From time to time, I was conscripted to help with the milking, which took some time from these large-uddered cows, whose teats had to be properly stretched. I made up my mind then that never again would I get involved in milking. That good resolution lasted less than thirty years. The cowman had cropped fair hair and a gentle Berkshire voice; I don't think he was very bright but my mother saw to it that everything was clean and shipshape, the cows well fed, groomed and washed down. The cowshed was just below the oak tree in the field to the far left of the house. Today that oak is about the only thing I can recognise in what were once the grounds of Cherwell. Chestnuts and elms, above all poplars, are such quick growers that one has lost the familiar shape even after ten years: was it this one or perhaps that which one knew so well? Oaks change slowly. Wolfson College almost touches it.

By now I was beginning to have slightly disturbing doubts about the Imperialist Conservative background to which my mother had accustomed me. Somehow a few Ruskin students had been invited to the house; it seems likely that they were miners or miners' sons and so would be welcomed. So much of my father's work was on mine safety and for my mother, miners, like fishermen, were 'different'; the class barrier dropped for them. We went up the river for a picnic in the usual flotilla. I had a shy student in the bows of my canoe and while I paddled I began asking him questions. In a little time he was telling me his life story and I was fascinated. This was pure Galsworthy! It started making holes in quite a lot of my assumptions. Then came the Oxford meeting when Lansbury and Larkin spoke and I was much shaken. Something was happening. But I was still a young lady and I had not even come out, so it would have been inappropriate for me to air my views. I would have been shut up. I might have been laughed at. I would have been caught out, made to say something silly and—yes, feminine. For there was certainly an overtone of male superiority and reasonableness, as against female passion and irrationality, though I don't think I recognised it as such. This has had something of a hang-over; I am still fairly easily silenced in a political argument, but not convinced. Early on I learnt that one. And I knew that I was beginning to sidle over from my mother's Tory side to my father's Haldane Liberalism, though I could still feel very disloyal if I didn't support her.

It appeared, up to 1914, that one could foresee one's whole life, and this was rather daunting. One would grow up, marry, have children (not that I cared much for this idea), live a North Oxford life with a house and servants and punctual meals, and nothing would ever change. Presumably 1914 was the last year when young people thought like that. As to a career for myself, that was very vague; my mother had wanted me to be a doctor, because that was what she had wanted for herself but had not been allowed to be. But I was not much attracted. I wanted to write, but somehow that was not sufficiently serious. Science was, and I was interested in certain aspects. But it did not seem to be enough. I wrote a semi-ironic so-called poem about that future, and yet it was not really *me* I wrote about; it was about imaginary grown-upness.

In North Oxford

Soon I must plait my hair in coils
And twist it tight about my head;
Low-necked and bare-armed I shall dance
In silken stuffs of green and red.

And I shall wear My Emeralds,
And I shall wear a Ruby Ring,
With all the many coloured world
About me for my pleasuring.

But ten years hence or maybe more,
A girl no longer, I shall dress
My hair a different, grown-up way
(And in ten years I shall have less).

And I shall wear Luxurious Furs,
And lovely satins, Hats with Plumes
For Photographs in Ascot Week,
And men will come to sketch my rooms—

For I shall buy Old Masters then,
The very modern art, of course,
With fine Crown Derby from the Sales.
And I shall back my Favourite Horse.

And then a husband—what a choice!
Statesman or artist, millionaire,
Duke, novelist, American,
Romantic burglar? I don't care.

Motors, a lovely sailing yacht,
An aeroplane, perhaps, by then . . .

I gave out after that, I couldn't see any further; at least it scans.
Here is a letter from Andrew Lang, dated 'St Andrews, Feb. 15':
no year, of course!

Dear Naomi,

I like your hexameters better than those of Mr Cotterill,
in a translation of the Odyssey; but *all* English (and German)
hexameters are naturally bad; as you will understand when
you can read Homer in Greek—and the sooner the better.
Conceive Sophocles trying to write Greek poetry in the metre
of 'Bonny Charlie's noo awa'. It is exactly the same as anybody
trying to write English hexameters. I did some when I was a
boy; but not being wholly lost, *I made them rhyme*. A little
girl died lately, about your age or younger, and her people
found that she had written several stories. I had to read one
of them today called 'Molly and Margaret', and I hope it will
be published; it was so funny and like small children. If you
never read a story of mine called 'The Monk of Fife' I would
like to send it to you, and if it bores you, you can chuck it into
the Cherwell, or give it to some poor child.

Yours very sincerely
A. Lang

There is a PS 'Love to the guinea pigs.'

I think this may well refer to a set of hexameters published in
the *Draconian* in 1911 by 'N. Haldane aged 13.' It appears to
be the thoughts of a ruined gambler:

Blessed is the cool of the night when the fever of gaming is over!
Oh, let me wander by nights thro' the streets, by the moon and
the starlight—
Naught but the streets is left for a penniless beggar and outcast
Etc., etc.

Oddly enough gambling is one of the temptations which I have never experienced, though, on the rare occasions when I have been to races or a casino, I have always won . . . though never more than five shillings!

But writing verses wasn't serious. Being a young lady was. This business of coming out involved several things: a difference in behaviour, which must no longer be silly or careless, a lengthening of skirts to ankle length and putting up one's long, maiden hair. The last was, to me, fiendishly difficult; I didn't want to be bothered with hairpins, nor did I think I looked any nicer with my hair bundled up behind. I was taken for lessons to a London hairdresser in one of the streets off Brompton Road, armed with tortoiseshell combs, one of which had to be stuck into the ends of one's hair and then wound over and over until finally the comb was pinned in at the back and one had a sizeable and heavy bun, which could be surmounted and decorated with another comb. Before long, however, I took to plaits wound round and round my head or in ear-phones. I doubt if this was a becoming style, but I simply was not thinking in those terms. It was easier and quicker, though even so they were always coming down. But silk-covered hairpins, a later invention, helped a lot. My mother still had her own hair cut short, which she had presumably done as a protest of a feminist kind some time in her twenties. But it was never suggested that I should imitate this.

By now I was regularly down for dinner at eight, and later, at sixteen, for dinner parties which on the whole I enjoyed very much. There were always a few undergraduates, and there was a lot of conversation, though I must take care to turn, halfway through dinner, that is to say at the end of the fish or *entrée* course (which we only had for real parties) to my other neighbour. I think the food must have been very dull, for I can't remember it. Chicken was still a treat, but probably tasted better than modern broilers. There was usually a choice, perhaps of roast, certainly of pudding, one of which was solid, the other frothy. In summer it would be gooseberry fool, strawberries and cream, or cherry pie. My father was sometimes bored or thinking of something utterly else which had been with him in study or laboratory. The family story has him gazing at the dish at his end of the table saying: 'Will anyone have any of this? It looks rather bad.'

But the dinner table looked nice, with crisp white damask linen and napkins folded into pleasing shapes. I had probably filled the big Sheffield plate wine coolers with suitable flowers: they looked marvellous with cow parsley and buttercups or ox-eye daisies, but good too with paeonies, which did well in our heavy-soiled garden, though they were only the ordinary ones. There was the large candelabra on a mirror stand, which, later on, at some point unaccountably disappeared. There were other candlesticks and the white candles were always new; there were the silver salt cellars and naturally the crested table silver. Fish knives were dreadfully middle-class; one ate fish with a fork. All had been polished by Miss Williamson and the current parlourmaid. The men had of course dressed for dinner; my father's stiff shirt creaked and bulged. He used to have trouble with his studs in the starched stud-holes, and he was bad at a white tie. It was essential that numbers of men and women should be even; this went on for as long as people gave formal dinner parties, but it got more and more difficult later on in the thirties as one's guests became more casual and perhaps more occupied. Whether or not Miss Blockey appeared depended on whether an extra woman was needed and if she came she would have the dullest partner. I was often quite sorry for her, though most of all when there had been an extra ticket for her at one of the 1914 Commem balls. At the last moment a cousin from Scotland turned up and poor old Blockywox was ruthlessly sacrificed, as unprotesting as Iphigeneia.

Sunday supper was less formal and always cold, often cold boiled chicken in a shiny white sauce or cold sirloin of English beef. There were more young people and it was much more fun. Nobody dressed for this, and I expect there were already some undergraduates who actually didn't own a dinner jacket! But at dinner parties, when the men were all dull black and white, the ladies were in shining silks and lace—though often with a shawl in Oxford unheated winters. They wore jewellery on their decolletées, an imposing necklace, sometimes a matching brooch and ear-rings. My generation did not have pierced ears; that was considered somewhat old-fashioned and barbaric. Most Scots ladies had a seed pearl necklace with broad, beautifully shaped leaves of mother-of-pearl, sewn scratchily with the small seed pearls. The one of my mother's necklaces which I liked best was enamel with tiny diamonds.

By this time smoking was not confined to the gentlemen or the eccentric female intellectual. Some people still considered it rather 'fast' but many ladies took an occasional cigarette, though my mother did not care for it, never smoked herself and would not have it in her sitting-room, especially my father's pipe, which, I must admit, was rather strong. Of course, I would never have been allowed to smoke, so naturally this was the only time in my life when I did take an occasional puff though I cannot say I ever really liked it. But most of my girl friends asserted themselves thus far, if no further.

Having a meal out was still a real thrill and rare. There was not much choice, at any rate in Oxford. Fuller's was best. But was the walnut cake with its thickly nutty embedding and the crisp-topped softness of the icing really as blissful as one remembers? Then there was the Cadena with the smell of coffee which I enjoyed years before I liked the taste, and the Oriental-style decor which I admired very much. Occasionally there was tea at the Randolph, very grand, and only with an occasional impor-tant visitor. In Edinburgh it was always one or another of the Princes Street shops with a view over to the gardens and the Castle if one got a window table. Cake stands were piled with dainties, scones were excellent. I doubt if synthetic cream had yet arrived and probably the main fat was real butter. Marge was still very lower-class and had not at all a nice taste or smell; it would never be bought even for cooking in most middle-class houses. I had never, of course, been inside a public house except for the inn at Sennen; one turned one's eyes away instinctively as from a public convenience.

I was in my mid-teens before I enjoyed going out to Oxford

parties, not that I could be asked to dinner myself, as I was not yet 'out'. But the notables were interesting, especially the Spoo, who, as Warden of New College, was the closest of the academics and occasionally even paid a call. Some of his sayings are undoubtedly made up (cherishing in one's bosom a half-warmed fish), but he certainly made some odd remarks, as to an English Jewish undergraduate, later a distinguished economist: 'I hope you will soon get on better with the European members of the College.' And he did some odd things, including, after dinner, saying to my mother that as it was rather dark on the stairs, he would give her some light, and went down switching everything off from the slippery dark oak of the Warden's lodging staircase. Dear Rosemary Spooner no doubt saved the situation. There was also his long conversation with the guy one Fifth of November. It was perhaps fortunate for my brother that his sight was bad. Jack took his turn with other scholars in reading the lesson at early Chapel, which indeed he rather enjoyed. I went along once and noticed the pyjama trousers under the surplice.

There were other senior New College dons, of whom the nicest was Joseph, the philosopher, who never managed to make the ancient philosophers palatable to the undergraduates doing Greats, but was much loved and enormously sympathetic. I remember, five years later, when I told him I was going to have a baby, as though it was the most astonishing thing in the world, how kindly he shared my wonder at this usual event. The senior Greats dons were more esteemed than scientists, historians or lawyers. There was Matheson—P. Mat.—whose lovely garden in Saville Road had enviable delphiniums, and Canon Rashdall—the Rasher—who was supposed to have said: 'I would like, just for once, to go to a Colchester oyster feast'— this in his deep, bubbly voice when talking, presumably, about hedonism. Professor Myres was about, when not archaeologising in more interesting places; many years later he sympathised with me when I changed my plough horses for a tractor, which could not be fed with the *cailleach*, the last sheaf. There was Ernest Barker who wrote a preface to my first book, *The Conquered*, to explain that it could be taken seriously as an illumination of history. Clearly a pleasant senior common room, with the unmarried members living in college, a short, moonlit walk across the quad. Among them were the younger dons, Heath, Cheeseman, Geoffrey Smith and the rest, of whom I cannot yet write without anger, when I think how they were killed in the useless trench fighting in 1915 and 1916.

And of course we lived in the world of the University characters and their wives, also formidable, especially the Smiths of Balliol. There were daughters of my own age; we met cautiously, I expect they were Liberals. There were the Lane Pooles, strong Imperialists, I think, and my remotish cousin, Robin Dundas of the House, who once marked a Greats candidate 'mud-bottom'. Naturally one expected one's friends to get Firsts or possibly 'good' Seconds.

All Oxford hospitality was in people's homes, where the wives counted, sometimes more than the husbands, but if we went to Edinburgh, we stayed at a hotel and visited cousins, including the one whose bones were always breaking and to whom my mother was devoted. I am sure poor Maya was beginning to consider a really nice Scots marriage for me, perhaps someone in the minor Tory landed aristocracy. She would have liked me to have land. Naturally she was pleased when we bought Carradale later on, but was aware that it was only the tail-end of an estate, so not quite land as it had seemed in her time. She made believe that the Cherwell fields were land in her sense and acquired some eight or ten acres more between us and the Marston Ferry road. She was now starting to sell the delicious Jersey milk and hers became the first grade A tuberculin tested herd in the south of England.

In London we sometimes stayed at Uncle Richard's house in Queen Anne's Gate, when he was not there. It was a beautiful eighteenth-century town house remodelled internally and decorated by Lutyens. Mrs Pinney, the housekeeper, was always nice to us and I enjoyed the books, collected editions in good bindings as well as the newest biographies and 'serious' novels. A good new novel was a recognised event in those days. Booksellers stocked it, had probably read it themselves and could recommend it. Or not! Reviewers had time and space to discuss one book. Sales of two or three thousand were quite good and brought in 'a modest competence'. Am I wrong to think that more depended on merit and less on packaging?

It was from Queen Anne's Gate in the summer of 1914 that I was allowed to go on one or two expeditions with Dick Mitchison. I am quite sure that by then my mother, if not my father, had been made aware that the elder of the Mitchison boys was seriously interested in the daughter of the Haldane house and that his intentions were strictly honourable. It is possible even that there had been some correspondence between the two mothers but of course I was considered much too young. I had not even properly 'come out' yet. But I think I must have been allowed the occasional daytime expedition so long as it was educational. Once, for instance, he took me to the Toynbee Hall Settlement where I think there had been a 'mission' run by New College.

South of the river was immediately different from the London I knew. But it was also vastly different from what it is now and much dirtier. There was no County Hall, no Festival Hall, not yet even an Old Vic. One was a stranger, stared at. The people who stared were another race, frightening. They wore dreadful rags of clothes. Some even had no shoes. I found myself shrinking, trying to get my breath and trying not to be so scared, but sure that Dick would protect me, if necessary by force, from the natives. I am sure, however, that I managed not to seem scared or behave in a silly 'feminine' way. We had both got so far as beginning to think that it was wrong that there should in London be people like this and something ought to be done about it. But that was as far as we had arrived and it was a very long way from revolution, or even the Fabian Society.

VI

Growing up into Science

What was my love-hate relation with science? Well, it went back some way, and there was always my father's lab in the background, though I never really understood the gas analysis apparatus, for example. But it became serious with the guinea pigs. I had started by keeping a few and gradually began to study them in a semi-scientific sense, listening to, identifying and copying their various squeaks and chitters, and seeing their relationship with one another and the whole pattern of guinea pig likes and dislikes. I even started taking notes. I certainly anthropomorphised too much, but I don't suppose anyone else has ever watched guinea pigs in this way. Scientifically they are an exploited race.

This went on for a couple of years and then Jack suggested that we should do serious genetics with them—Mendelism, as it was called after the newly discovered papers of the Abbé Mendel, on whose statue (is it still there?) I once, years later on, laid a wreath. I became quite keen and we went ahead with a whole range of two-compartment guinea pig hutches, so much nicer for them than today's wire cages in lab animal houses, built along the hedge by the side of the path that went past the tennis court and down to the boathouse. I of course did the feeding and cleaning, though somebody else must have done it during the holidays. It was an unscientific diet compared with the measured and, one would think, uninteresting, standard ration of the modern lab guinea pig, but I watched to see what they liked. They throve, reared big families and were relatively long-lived. I squeezed milk from the teats of one of my loved ones, so as to taste it, but it was rather nasty, and I understood their sex life, with its genuine likes and dislikes, so well that I thought there was nothing about sex that I didn't know. Females accepted and suckled the babies of those females whom they liked, rejecting those whose mothers they disliked. But is 'like' and 'dislike' the correct way of considering this? There are probably other reasons.

After a while I became something of an expert and was written to for advice on guinea pig habits and ailments. We got some new kinds, as we wanted to see not only how colour and brindling was inherited, but also long and short hair, and the whorls of show guinea pigs, though I never entered the show world. Occasionally we found a mutation, for instance a small extra toe, and followed that up. Perhaps the stud books we kept still exist somewhere: I named every guinea pig appropriately, many of them after the famous scientists of the day.

But by and by we began to realise that our results were not working out on expected Mendelian lines. We had in fact happened on what was then called linkage and later cross-over, but as nobody had yet got onto the chromosome structure it was very puzzling. But, luckily for me, there was little of the mathematics that seems to be necessary for modern genetics and none I couldn't manage. For a long time the physical structure of chromosomal cell division was theoretical and some of the guesses were far from correct. When Morgan's book, *The Physical Basis of Heredity*, came out, it was deeply exciting; I remember reading it in great gulps curled up on the school-room sofa and seeing how much it explained. But at first we were puzzled by some of our results; we decided to enlarge the experiments to include mice and rats; these were kept in the University animal house and complicated by the considerable ability of the mice to escape out of their cages at crucial moments in their sex life. The rats, on the other hand, bit; Frances helped with them, having vaguely scientific interests.

I never got fond of the rats, intelligent as they were, in the same way that I did with my guinea pigs. Once, going out to feed them, I heard the scream for help, ran and found Titi, whose cage I always left open so that she could forage, her hackles up, facing a weasel, while her family scuttled for shelter in the hedge—I can see them still, small brown panicked lumps among the ivy and wild violet leaves. I snatched Titi up and the weasel looked at me with wicked little eyes, humped ready to jump. Knowing they go for the neck vein I was frightened, but held Titi tightly covered in my hands, feeling her poor little heart racing, and kicked out at the weasel with my solid school-boy shoes. It went away and I put Titi down to call to her family, gather them up and get back into her hutch. One had to look out, too, for owls and hawks, especially if any of my flock were in open-topped runs on the croquet lawn grass. Occasionally we had to kill one that had been wounded, in the inner lab under a bell glass connected to the gas tap, always something traumatic for me. But I didn't mind doing PMs. If any pregnant females died or were killed it was essential to look at the colours of the unknown litter.

At the animal house I got to know some of the 'lab boys', skilled technicians some of them. They helped me later when I was doing science prelims, and for a long time it was thought on that level that I would have made a good scientist. Maybe. The first published paper I had my name on was a joint one on colour inheritance in rats, which was fairly simple. As an initial, *N.H.*, *six years old, four feet high, weighing 25·2 kilos and with rather well developed lung area*, I come, however, into one of my father's and Miss Fitzgerald's joint papers, as do my brother and various friends from the Dragon School. Later on, living in London, in Chelsea, within walking distance of the Lister Institute, I thought I could do some work on *Gammarus*, and had a shelf of labelled finger bowls full of families of these rather unattractive creatures in the bathroom. But it didn't work out. I had to give up scientific practice, and instead, write.

The guinea pig results were never clear-cut and we had so many factors to consider; besides they do not breed as fast as mice. Once we bought an apparently pink guinea pig, but the colour wore off. I would do a prowl from time to time among the cages in the market in case there was anything interesting, an extra fold on the ear, for instance. The market was always fun, though perhaps a bit dirtier in those days than it is now; I think Tyrell had most of the animals in his shop. We had our scientific eye already on the many breeds of domestic fowl, and there were vast areas of flowering plants to consider. But with the war, from 1914 onwards, there was a cutting back in the guinea pig population, both in numbers and in our interest. Later on my mother kept rabbits for eating in some of the empty hutches.

I was of course constantly in and out of my father's laboratory, but without much understanding of what the experimental work was actually about. At this period much of my father's work was in connection with mining, for the Institute of Mining Engineers. He had, indeed, worked closely with them for many years, receiving the Greenwell Medal, perhaps one of the ugliest ever to be designed, in 1904, and later becoming the President; he was still likely to be called for if there was a mine disaster, and he was director of the Colliery Owners' research laboratory at Doncaster—later transferred to Birmingham. So mining was always very close to us all. But this work, originally no doubt practical, in the sense that it was saving miners from death by breathing poisonous gases, had turned inevitably to the basic questions of the physiology of breathing and the functions of the lungs, so much more complex than they had once seemed. Breathing, both normal and under various kinds of experimental conditions, was constantly being watched and measured. As so often happens, 'pure' science was necessary in order to make practice really effective.

My father was writing one paper after another in conjunction with various people, Boycott, Damant, Butterfield, Lorrain-Smith, Gillies Priestley and others, but especially C. G. Douglas, some on such things as testing for carbon monoxide in mines, others, for instance, on the degree of absorption of oxygen by the lungs, studied in his own laboratory. But this was varied by excursions into photometry; he was still doing official work as a Gas Referee as well. He gave up University teaching in 1913. Sometimes he went over to Doncaster to test mine rescue apparatus, some of which was worse than useless, and to design

Above Dick, Gervas, Jack and me in *Prisoners of War*, 1914
Below Aldous as Charon, Lewis as Dionysos in *The Frogs*, 1914

Saunes Bairos. The cast in New College cloister. My mother is standing behind me in the third row with Lewis and Dick to the left and Aldous and Trev behind her. Miss Blockey is third from the left and Frances is on the extreme right in the second row

better ones. This meant train journeys, during which he could settle down to think and work, as one cannot do nowadays, driving a car.

In 1911 he wrote six papers, five in 1912. Some are Royal Society transactions, and there is a Discussion on Vitalism in the *British Medical Journal*—for he always kept one foot in the philosophers' camp. Everything was written out in ink and the papers mounted up in piles on tables and carpet. I can't imagine that he would have been comfortable with a typewriter; he was extremely suspicious even of a slide rule. But I doubt if he ever worried much about the business side of life; that would have been taken care of in Edinburgh by the family firm of Writers to the Signet.

I might be sent in to say that somebody wanted to see him or that he had a telephone call. I would talk to Mavro or Gillies or stroke the experimental mice—or catch one if it got lost under a bench. Sometimes I did a bit of washing up, or watching what was happening in one of the large metal chambers where experiments on respiration were going on; occasionally I was left with the instruction that if the experimenter—usually my father—fell over unconscious, I was to undo the door, pull him out and do artificial respiration. But this never happened.

Work here began at a reasonable hour. My father tended to have a late, solid British breakfast, the eggs or kidneys kept hot in a silver dish, and miss lunch. At tea-time he emerged, often in term-time to a dozen or so young people, to whom he would be absentmindedly pleasant. Work went on after dinner until very late, long after my bedtime, which was still almost always around nine. Towards midnight the tray would be taken in to the study with milk and plum cake. I notice in one of his papers, in which meals were noted, the constant '12·30 glass of milk'. Beyond that, I would think that Uffer and probably one or two of the team might still be working till three in the morning. It was, I am sure, a happy time for them. It meant a great deal to my father to have his son beginning to work with him. Their first joint paper was in 1912, when Jack was only nineteen. He was reading Greats, following Maths Mods; his First was almost taken for granted, so he had time for scientific discussion as well and the detailed talking over of experimental work. Aldous Huxley, who was entirely part of the household, must have been taking it all in. Later on, out comes some of it with Lord Edward Tantamount in *Point Counter Point*.

My father had perhaps built too much on becoming Professor of Physiology: to some he was the obvious choice. It had brought him out of deep depression after that earlier election when his uncle, out of deeply principled antinepotism, failed to support him, and Gotch got the Waynflete Chair (and Gotch was certainly not a great scientist) that New College gave him a Fellowship. He had a deep love and loyalty towards the College; he enjoyed the romantic aspect, the candles and the silver, and he was very fond of his younger colleagues. They, as well as the undergraduates and Rhodes scholars, came to tea now and then.

Understandably he resigned as Reader after Sherrington became Professor—and what a good teacher Sherrington was!—and there were always complications about lab space. But his connection with the Physiology Department still went on for a time. Florence Buchanan—Aunt Florence—a great physiologist in her difficult way, had to be championed; her detached retina deteriorated, though her brain remained active; today's lasers could probably have stabilised her retina and given her many more working years. University politics are always full of vicious in-fighting and presumably the fact that Oxford was particularly well padded against the conflicts which were coming up, both in less prosperous parts of Britain and in the outside world, meant that academic quarrels were very bitter and in-turned.

After his own laboratory at Cherwell was built, he finally ceased working altogether at the University Physiology Laboratory, although, for many people and especially the technicians, 'Dr Haldane's room' was still there. Some of his things, including the big balance, are still in the new building, and used; his presence remains, his papers are classics.

66

The one who suffered was C. G. Douglas; as a University lecturer he worked in the Physiology Laboratory. But his heart was a mile away, in the other laboratory across the Parks in North Oxford, with my father. Perhaps he was a little overshadowed —one doesn't know. But his and my father's minds worked admirably together on the respiratory regulation problems which they did so much to put into order. It left us all with an interest in breathing—I still find myself playing games with 'forced breathing'.

An increasingly familiar figure had been Yandell Henderson of Yale, full of enthusiasm, my notion of what an American should be like, perhaps the sender of my favourite American journal. It was he who had first brought Pike's Peak into the picture, I believe after a casual remark by my father at some conference that if only there was a high altitude mountain with a comfortable hotel at the top—earlier work had been done in mountain huts in conditions of considerable difficulty—he would go and investigate blood and respiration changes there. Yandell Henderson's immediate answer was Pike's Peak in Colorado.

The first expedition, in which Douglas and Barcroft took part, was an international one to the Peak of Tenerife. Here the preliminary questions and work started off, and the next year, 1910, came the expedition to Pike's Peak, with my father, Douglas, Yandell Henderson and Schneider of Colorado. This was the summit party, but they did not take Miss Fitzgerald, surely as eminent a physiologist as the rest, but—a woman. She, however, did equally valuable work, by herself, in the smaller hills. I remember her only vaguely, and as someone a little bit alarming; she outlived my father by some forty years. The Pike's Peak expedition is only in my mind because of my father's stories afterwards, especially of the visitors to Pike's Peak getting out of the carriages of the mountain railway, overwhelmed with mountain sickness. This struck both my father and me as delightfully funny, so I always enjoyed hearing him tell that one to the tea-time undergraduates.

The deep-sea diving work which had started in the Kyles of

Bute was being continued at Portsmouth with Guy Damant. Exact instructions were laid down for Admiralty divers and strictly followed. The tables are still in use and unchallenged for scientific accuracy, though diving has gone so much deeper and the free-lance divers who hire themselves out in the North Sea and elsewhere do not follow the Haldane table and consequently get bends and all too often die in great pain.

There was, then, this type of background during the years after the Dragon School when I was at home. The words were familiar, however little I really understood: alveolar air, lactic acid, the Haldane gas apparatus, the Douglas bag. There were not only the regular workers, but my old love Teddy Boycott, now a father, entirely grown-up, and then Barcroft, and the Copenhagen physiologists, the hours of talk going on in the study and the smell of pipe smoke coming out. But was that going to be my life?

VII

Oxford and Scotland

But have I any reason to think I was a budding scientist? Not really. Or a budding anything else serious or tangible? I disliked history. I was no good at languages. If I was anything, it was a good observer, not only of guinea pigs and wild plants, but also of people, and especially of people in relation to myself, a not uncommon teenage interest.

This watching of people was what I was doing with my brother, the person I loved best—though I had never formulated this. It was a deeply exciting relationship and part of it was meeting his friends, and our intellectual discussions in which I was always trying to make it into the undergraduate world. There were those wonderful teas in New College. Jack had rooms in the new buildings almost opposite the flowering cherry and in those uncrowded days an undergraduate had sitter and bedder, looked after by a scout who saw that the fire was going nicely, and we always had splendid mounds of thick buttery toast with Gentleman's Relish and then perhaps a Fuller's cake, of which I could and did eat slice after slice.

I suppose I was fairly attractive even at fifteen or sixteen, but if I was with Jack I could be unchaperoned. Elsewhere I, like the other girls, including female students, must be accompanied by a reputable female: for me it was usually my mother, to whom due deference was paid. Sometimes it was Miss Blockey, but my mother liked undergraduates and did much pro-Empire propaganda, which they were polite about, whether or not they accepted it. Any male over thirteen was potentially dangerous. One would think this must have been embarrassing for the chaperones, but it was never mentioned, so perhaps it wasn't. These social habits were taken for granted, like equally strange ones in India or Japan. I remember, rather later, there were great hunts for tactful 'chaps' who would stay in their corner whatever went on. Up to a fairly decorous point, that is! There was no necking or petting of the modern kind. But even at sixteen I wasn't really irked by chaperonage. The excitement was in the conversation between young people, spiced with clever quotations and local jokes, or witty remarks treasured.

These were still the days of the Bloods who had, it seems, dominated young University life for a long time but had only lately come to be resented actively, instead of being accepted as the kind of thing that happens in a class society. The Bullingdon Club and other Blood organisations had been behaving very badly in the early years of the century, in what would now be called a fascist way. That would be incorrect; they had no overt political philosophy, though many of their enemies held leftish views; they probably, but not necessarily, were Tory material. But they had a class arrogance which was becoming less and less tolerable in a society like Oxford, which was slowly changing into something fairly mobile class-wise. They had broken into the rooms of intellectuals, destroying books or pictures, knocking the owners about. They had torn up the manuscript—years of work— of a don they did not favour. They were forever lighting bonners in the quads into which they threw things they disapproved of. No point in going into names now; what was done was done. The College authorities were, by and large, unable or scared to control or discipline the Bloods, many of whom came from aristocratic families with quite a lot of political and social power. Some of them died heroically in the early months of the war, perhaps fulfilling themselves. That made their actions at Oxford no less detestable.

There was no sympathy in our house for the Bloods. Aristocrats they might be, but gentry they were not. My father would come out black angry at their anti-intellectualism every time the Bullingdon Club went in for one of their antics—when they

ducked someone in Mercury or smashed down the door of someone else who had sported his oak and was attempting to work.
They tended to be several against one. They were mostly English
and they admired one another. Plato might have admired them in
the same breath that he admired the Spartans.

But as I remember now there was always an undercurrent of
University gossip and giggle wherever one went. There were
endless funny stories, normally against the Proctors and their
'bull dogs', though also criticism of the Bloods for having scared
the guts out of the 'bull dogs' who had then turned aside to catch
some relatively minor offender from, say, Jesus (or Jaggers as we
would have said). My brother was an expert climber in and out of
College and tended to be somewhat boastful about it. Once, when
he had been gated, he climbed in and out every night, contemptuous
of the 'bull dogs'. Unfairly I thought, after the war when he
became a don at New College, he closed some of the easier routes,
in the interest, he said, of a fine old sport.

That was the University side. But sometimes and happily I
went for long walks with Trev Huxley; the Huxleys were so
nearly counted as kin that chaperonage was not considered necessary. We looked for birds and rare wild flowers. He tried to teach
me to differentiate bird song, but my piano lessons had not helped
me over this and I could not manage it except for the obvious,
so that I could never spot an exciting bird as well as I could a
plant. Mostly we went across the river and up towards Elsfield.
I suppose this is all now post-Nuffield suburbs, including perhaps
the damp woodlands where wild columbines grew and the usual
splendid mixture of orchis. We walked from our house by way
of the ferry, crossing our own lower meadow, often squashy
with an open field drain spectacular with golden marsh marigolds,
then over the fence and across two more water meadows, never
ploughed up but perpetually grazed or enclosed for hay. Between
them there was a fascinating mixed hedge, with a kind of path
through the middle after one had jumped the ditch; here in autumn
there were spindleberry bushes and boughs full of juicy sloes.

Then we cut down to the ferry and rang the bell; for a penny or two we were taken over, both of us pulling on the wire along with the ferryman. Then up past the inn, and on the stiled path to Old Marston with its solid village houses of golden-grey stone, on to the eastern by-road where one rarely met any traffic. Usually we turned off about the foot of Elsfield hill onto one of the many field paths, and there was endless interest and conversation, Huxley jokes and limericks. When in August 1914, Trev killed himself, it was for me and many another the end of the old life and the beginning of the personal evil and loss which we were going to experience.

What were we after, then? We were light-hearted on the whole, especially over politics. There was a strike by the Oxford tram drivers and conductors, whose wages would seem ludicrous by modern standards. A fleet of strike-breaking buses was laid on and we all went gaily into action, chanting, 'Buckell's blackleg buses!'—and trying to hamper them as far as possible. My brother caused an obstruction in Cornmarket by chanting (in a later letter to me he wrote 'singing'—but no!) the Athanasian Creed. I rather think the strikers won. But we were not deeply involved, so far, though others in the University were, including G. D. H. Cole and his friends who were already politically serious. Supporting the strikers was a pleasantly anti-Establishment gesture, not really more, and was scarcely effective against my mother, since not only did she somewhat sympathise with the strikers, but disliked Buckell, who was an arrogant townee. On the other hand there was her indignation at having to lick insurance stamps for the servants, forced onto employers by that odious Lloyd George.

All of this happened against a background of Oxford as it was then, a place of uncrowded, unhurried streets, still definitely University: handsome young men sauntering in white flannels and boaters or running in longish, flapping shorts, sometimes with College scarves and blazers or even academic dress at exam times, the women students on the whole earnest looking in their long skirts, only perhaps to be spotted in book shops, or about to play tennis. One main difference from now was the comparative

72

absence of foreign accents. A few refugees settled during World War One, but the great influx was before and during World War Two, starting with the Jewish flight from Hitler. Oxford has always been a favourite nesting ground for au pair girls. Equally it has been a place where the elderly feel at home. Lately, on a visit to the House, I looked in at the Cathedral. It seemed to me that exactly the same congregation was drifting in, wearing much the same clothes and hats and expressions. But could it have been? Had they somehow been in cold storage since my youth? Surely I couldn't be that age myself? Would a teenager have equated them with me? I suppose so, but duck away from my logical supposition.

During my teens the cattle market was still being held and there were definitely bucolic types around with thick Oxfordshire accents, though not yet, of course, the Cowley incomers. The colleges and older buildings were much as now, perhaps even gayer with window boxes in summer, and where Banbury Road branches off there was a pretty little stone-built dame school on the right hand side, to which my brother went for a short time at around four, until his precocity was too much for them. In the triangle where Parks Road joins, which is now full of the peculiar shapes of science buildings, there was a nursery garden and a shabby little greenhouse with steps. It would, in season, have boxes of lobelias, marguerites and so on. It is clear that North Oxford front gardens were very dull compared with today. It was still privet, spotty laurel and laurestinus, with the most ordinary spring bulbs. There were pink horse chestnuts, double red hawthorn, double pink cherry, laburnum, but very little in the way of interesting *malus* or *prunus* varieties, only the standard blue *Jackmanii* clematis, only the double red paeony, little variety of iris. Nobody then would have dared to plant a magnolia, still less a camellia, although the colleges were beginning to be more advanced. But the gardening interest and industry of today were only just beginning. Both food and gardens have become much better since they have been cooked or planted by their actual owners.

Moving up to North Oxford, the entrance to Parktown was exactly the same, though the gentlemen's convenience was rather more shrouded. The Dicey's hedge was higher and wilder. On the other side there was Gee's, the smart greenhouse, that always had palms and cyclamens and hothouse grapes, which one occasionally bought for invalids, exactly the same as now. There was a post office next to it in those days, one of those nice post offices which are also small shops with a stand of post cards, which one sent to relatives in New Zealand. None of today's anti-mugging devices were necessary; small post office tills still went unrobbed, so everything was nice and open and friendly. We did a lot of shopping in North Parade and Mr Bennet still made my father's lace-up boots, working at home in his own little house which then seemed small and poor, but has probably by now been tarted up into a highly desirable middle-class residence. People had their special lasts at the bootmaker and if they acquired a corn, a model of it could be added to the last.

I suppose the river has altered rather less, though doubtless the willows are kept more in order. Are they still pollarded for use or only out of old habit? My brother rowed in College Torpids in the Lent Term, but he was a heavyweight and had to have a special oar built for him, which, even so, occasionally cracked, so it was doubtful whether the extra horse power he put into his rowing made up for the extra weight. He never got into a College eight. However, Torpids, the earlier race, also meant going into training, with fairly strict (but probably inaccurate) dieting, as well as a Spartiate abstention from this and that. But after the race all ended with a bonner and a drunk; College ale was strong. Sometimes too, it might finish up with what was known as a bit of skirt, but by no means always. There wasn't the same easy opportunity and Jack did not go in for the tobacconist's assistant type who was more or less available; in fact up to 1914 his sexual experience, like mine, was practically non-existent, except for erotic verse and guinea pig watching.

But with a certain alcoholic stimulus, what he did was to speak exclusively in blank verse of a classical, Shakespearean kind. This was well known and admired. Of course English speech goes very readily into this form, which one must be somewhat careful to avoid (note the last seven words). Note also the 'free verse' forms into which words spoken under deep stress fit themselves, for instance in *The Catonville Nine*. But during all my brother's life alcohol, even in quite small doses, seemed to release verse centres. Later it tended to be long quotes from Lucretius, Dante or, later still, the Sanskrit scriptures. Even sometimes the Bible. I myself usually, but not, I fear, always, keep this longing to spout verse inside my mouth.

Verse, yes, the running of words inside one's head, often interfering with thought or sensible planning or listening to other people. For years, and long beyond this period of my life, one of my favourite games was capping verse in its various forms: taking the last word of a line and finding another line which includes it (an easier version just takes the first letter of the last word and begins the next line with it), or simply finding a line whose author the other players cannot guess. Real highbrows can of course play this in several languages. As one gets older one tends to go back to Hymns A and M or nursery rhymes. Jack and I played this and other word or poetry games in the course of long walks at Cloan during the summer holidays in Scotland, up past the summer houses or along to where the glen flattens out into ferns and birch scrub with wild pansies and blue milkwort, perhaps even over the old hill road to Glen Devon.

We went for long walks, on which my father could still easily out-walk me. It wasn't until I was in my twenties that I found I was tending to out-walk him; but that was after his work on poison gases in World War One and his lungs were beginning to give. Almost every summer we used to have an expedition across the strath to Ben Vorlich; this had to be arranged when the Cloan car was available to take us somewhere near the foot. It was here that I was stricken with such fearful jealousy that it was like a sudden illness. The Stracheys were staying at Cloan. Amabel had a magnificent, enviable mane of red hair and appeared to me to be superbly confident, almost grown-up. And Jack asked her to be his climbing companion! Amabel tells me that actually she was feeling a bit shy and was somewhat surprised by this offer from a young man who rather scared her. Nor did they have much conversation on Ben Vorlich. Quite likely the invitation was an act of genuine good manners by Jack. Or was it perhaps that he was a little bored with me always tagging along?

I climbed with someone else and raging passion inside me. It was a horrible day. Probably I was thoroughly nasty to everyone. When I calmed down I managed to recognise that this which had come at me was the opposite of delight, was due to asserting ownership over another person and was the worst possible way of binding oneself to the Wheel. I never experienced the same emotion later on, perhaps because when I began to feel it I recognised it, tried to understand, rationalise and sublimate it. However it made me highly critical of any story or play which had sexual jealousy as its motive, including of course *Othello* and several other of the major Elizabethans. Intellectual and professional jealousy was more interesting and intelligible, perhaps sometimes justified, but usually it also led to wrong action. Or so it seemed to me.

We went on going up to my grandmother at Cloan every summer and often at New Year; things changed slowly. There were constant 'improvements' both at Cloan and Foswell. That kind of thing was not so expensive, relatively, as it is now; everything was done by the local builder and joiner. Year after year I ran out and bit off the tips of the tropaeolum flowers that shone in brilliant scarlet on the dark holly leaves of the big hedge, and sucked the honey. Year after year I gathered up the peacock feathers. In late April I picked the tiny delicate flowers of the wood sorrel, white pencilled with white, touched them with fingers and tongue, at last ate them. In summer I ate half-ripe plums and green apples, the last, late, slug-nibbled strawberries. The gong went for meals. I trailed books all over the house. I dropped my clothes on the floor; someone picked them up and washed them and they were doubtless ironed with heavy flat-irons off the stove. Bits of rhymes came into my head. Tremendous sunsets flamed over the hills on the far side of the strath; I tried to find words for them. I swung between irrational fears and sudden delights. In sparkling brightness after a shower I saw in a single raindrop hanging from a rhododendron leaf the whole thing reflected as in an eye and it threw me into a turmoil of pleasure.

Today I get great pleasure from garden flowers and especially good rhododendrons—Cloan is too high and chilly for the really classy ones!—but now it is not simple and absolute but full of expertise and questioning: how did they manage on this soil? Where did they get it and how much did it cost? This might be a *Gigha* hybrid. That has the *Loderi* scent but it looks more like a *Griffithianum* parentage. Or, more simply (but for a shrub rather than a rhododendron!): nobody's looking—if I just take a small cutting—but all this is being an elderly gardener, and in the back of her mind the thought of how many more Springs, not an adolescent overwhelmed by a particular kind of beauty, yet about to let it sweep away so as to be overwhelmed by another. The inexpert, non-intellectual pleasure of the senses: that goes.

Inside Cloan the senses had less to feed on. The pictures on the landings and corridors did not change. They tended to be monochrome reproductions of old masters; I especially disliked Saint Augustine and his Mum. In the drawing-room there were some quite pleasant water colours, but also framed photographs. King Edward, signed for Uncle Richard, in his silver mount. Later there was Einstein on the steps of Queen Anne's Gate. I found these fascinating, as also the cartoons of Uncle Richard which increasingly covered the walls between dining-room and smoking-room. But in general my aesthetic tastes were undeveloped and I found it essential that a picture should be about something or someone recognisable and interesting; I didn't start knowing what pictures are really about until many years later.

People didn't change much. Granniema in her eighties was rather more upstairs in her room but one felt her presence in the house. One was welcomed by the same housemaid who tidied up after one as before. The Foswell family, the 'Fossils', were always there, a compact bunch, perhaps sometimes resenting the way that I or other children were sent up there from Cloan, deeply aware that they were the ones who knew and understood the real, factual place, who knew where to find the birds and the fish, who were aware of exact growth and change. But they had to accept us and the young Belloc Lowndes's, for instance, or the young Inges. I felt that Elsie, my senior, was the completely competent and admirable one: 'One of the horses bolted for a mile with Archie but Elsie managed to get beside and stop him.' Or again: 'Elsie is an expert motorist now and she drove us to Dunblane the other day.' My brother did some riding on a horse called Sir Edward but I never felt I wanted to ride after my broken leg.

We went on longer walks every year, especially over to Glen Devon by the hill road. One of my letters goes: 'We walked over to the Scott Moncrieffs on Wednesday across the hills. It was awfully jolly particularly coming back in the dark with an inadequate lantern which went out half way. The road was frightfully bad—most of the way merely a channel for a small burn but we waded through the water where we could see it because there might be all sorts of pitfalls which we could not see on the dry road while the water was merely wet.' There was Craig Rossie and the burn below it. 'We went to the Black Swelch one day. It was looking splendid, the brown flood water gurgling up against the rocks and banging the stones about.'

Whenever I was at Cloan without my mother I duly wrote to her almost every day. By this time my handwriting had become (unfortunately) much what it is now. There are longish letters of description written on Cloan paper, which my mother kept, just as I have been unable not to keep letters from my own children. 'We thought the big spruce in front of the house was coming down on Tuesday night and went to the door to watch it fall. It was rocking and straining like anything but it did not go. The lower part of the high wood and most of the low wood

is absolutely "squishé" and they are cutting up the wood.'
This was in New Year, 1912, when Jack and I were both there.
I certainly remember that chaos of uprooted and broken spruces
blocking the winding paths—or do I remember one of the several
other times this happened?

Clearly my mother had written a fussy letter, for I write: 'My
hair is all right and Burser [she must have been the then head
housemaid] brushes it almost always and ties it in the evening.'
Then at the end, 'I think there is going to be a fancy dress dance
in the barn on the 3rd. I think I will see if I can manufacture a
hoop and wear Granniema's old dress.' I don't remember if I
did but I do remember Granniema's old dress with its marvellously
narrow waist which later I inherited and lent to a daughter—and
never saw again. Fancy dress was always a delightful thing in
those days: much less necessary now when everything can be
fancy. Then it was one's only chance to wear—just possibly!—
trousers, doubtless with a baggy blouse decently covering the
flies.

A few days later my mother had another letter from me: 'Can
we have our stockings the night we come back? I have a Venus of
Milo two inches high and did you remember the bullseyes? They
are in the top drawer of the glass top cupboard in the sitting-
room.' Yes, there was the revolting little Venus of Milo in white
ceramic which both my brother and I liked so much. It was, like
the Christmas stockings, a bit of non-grown-upness.

Every year there were August shoots at Cloan and Foswell.
My brother took a gun and was a reasonably good shot. But,
like many another, he never shot again for pleasure after the
1914 war. I was once taken into one of the butts, but was so upset
by the slaughter of the grouse (although I helped to eat them
later) that I wasn't taken again. Picnics happened at the edge of
the moor above Foswell, all females hatted against the sun,
the men large in tweeds, keepers and gillies discreetly eating, and
doubtless drinking, in the background, and an exquisite tiny
burn over-hung by miniature cliffs over which grass of Parnassus
and bell heather hung from moss beds. But for the Foswells, a

79

burn, even a small one, was a hiding place for trout. Archie, three years younger than me, would go down and guddle trout if Uncle Richard had some specially important guest and none had been caught with rod and line. One can see in his books the same passionate feeling as mine for certain aspects of natural beauty. Yet it was half a century before we could talk about it with one another. Nothing is better eating than a grilled brown trout. But I was beginning to have vaguely humanitarian leanings about blood sports. That was in the air, at least for ladies.

By now I was beginning to listen to the grown-up conversations at Cloan, though unhappily many of them ended in the library, which was also the smoking-room and gentlemen's ground after meals, even if I had been curled up reading there all morning. Sometimes I had to trust Jack to tell me the end of stories, like Uncle Richard's legal one about the lady who was domiciled in Jersey and the St Bernard dog. I was already beginning to pride myself on never being shocked, though sometimes I was.

Although this was the full period of suffragette militancy, some of it, I would have thought, very much up my street, it did not affect me at all, and this must have meant that I didn't hear it talked about. With the dullness of newspapers and of course no radio, one could easily miss what was going on. Yet both my mother and Aunt Bay were keen feminists and certainly believed that the vote was important. But both were anti-militant, deeply shocked by behaviour which they considered both unwomanly and unladylike. Aunt Bay had been immensely active in public works, a member of various royal commissions, a trustee of the Carnegie United Kingdom Trust, and so on; she was to be made the first woman JP in Scotland. But I doubt if the Pankhursts would have been received either at Cherwell or Cloan.

I was becoming more interested in our Perthshire neighbours, though the Haldanes of Cloan had cut themselves off to some extent by supporting the Free Church, the people's church. However our cousin, Bishop Chinnery Haldane, was also a splendid eccentric, much loved in his vastly scattered Argyll diocese on which he spent all his salary, where he walked across country, swimming lochs (or so the story goes) and walking into any cottage at night for hospitality, where (again the tale is) he took the peculiar action of opening the windows. Long after, in the sixties, when I stood as Labour candidate for Kinlochleven in the County Council elections, I was billed as the Bishop's niece, and many a good Labour and Church of Scotland voter had his photograph in the best room.

By now I was expected to go to kirk on a Sunday from time to time, walking of course. Afterwards we had singed sheep's head in barley and Uncle Richard would tease me by picking out an eye and offering it. But with luck one could get cold beef instead. There was one Sabbath when I was so cruelly affected by giggles which had to be suppressed that I ached for the rest of the day. Earlier, one of the party had torn a hole in his trousers—fairly high up—the text was new cloth on old garments. Of such material are giggles made; I was no more immune than any other teenager.

At Cloan we had hothouse grapes for dessert, of which one was allowed a small branch, usually cut by the butler. Here again, everyone dressed for dinner, though Uncle Richard often wore a velvet smoking jacket, the height, I thought, of almost decadent luxury. The nicest things to eat were apt to be in short supply. I could never get enough of the broad beans which had always, of course, been skinned by the kitchen maid. As another matter of course we always had excellent oat cakes and there was comb honey for tea, with hot scones, smaller and crustier than our Oxford ones. Any house to which one went for tea would certainly have hot scones, muffins, crumpets or tea-cakes in a covered china or silver dish. But crumpets were always 'bought'. At Cloan Uncle Richard sometimes had separate little snacks of red herring or German delicacies. Once or twice during the holidays I would go down to Auchterarder with Aunt Bay, to Eadie the baker, for shortbread and their big tea biscuits which were particularly good. We still visited the sick and old, but no longer, I think, went to the Poor House, which by then may well have been much improved.

There was more machinery now on the farms and fewer horses, though the yard was still pleasantly full of horse noises at lowsing time. But I think already there was a steam threshing mill going round. Aunt Bay was pushing the garden out, making new little fountains, planting more apple trees and yew hedges by the dogs' cemetery, and the fine sweeping border just before the start of the upper walk along the glen. Foswell was somewhat rebuilt, becoming the charming house it is now.

I took little interest in the farming or the forestry, though it was always interesting to see a side of the glen clear-felled and pouring up leaves and flowers into the new sunlight between the resin-oozing stumps. The wild roses were different from the Oxford and Berkshire ones, though Bentham and Hooker did not really distinguish them; the ripe hips tasted slightly different, too. We hunted for blaeberries, but seldom found enough to bring proudly back. But always the things I really wanted were the walks with Jack, the throwing out of a feeler for the poetry game and between questions letting the words and phrases run in colour over one's inner background.

VIII

Class and Prejudice

It is difficult to reconstruct the standards and fine distinctions of the society in which I grew up. One was supposed to know them all in some subconscious way. Occasional echoes flit across my mind still. It was clear to me for instance that my mother felt that there were sometimes guests at Cloan who were not what she herself approved of, and this meant that her in-laws were either insensitive or not themselves quite her own social class— I fear the latter, always excepting Granniema. Or was it simply that they were Liberals, which in itself meant lower standards? But it was very puzzling for me. Maya had a great covering word: 'undesirable'. This might mean either a wrong social class or bad habits in our own (or higher?—no, we did not admit that, except for Royalty who were part of the Empire): things like drinking or fornication or showing off. Or being foreigners. But this wasn't clear. Danes, for instance, were quite all right. So were Austrians. But Germans were certainly among the undesirables, and there was a certain Germanic bias among the Haldanes. My father had few French colleagues and on the rare occasions when he met them, he tended to address them as '*Ach, mein liebe Kollege!*' I think they might have been suspected of flirtatiousness. As for Americans, they also were rather suspect, except for my Keatinge cousins—on my mother's side! But I myself saw them in the witty and memorable terms of some American magazine—was it perhaps the first years of *Vanity Fair?*—which for a year or two floated into the house, perhaps a gift. I always seized this, if possible, to have a first read, especially if the issue appeared likely to be disapproved of!

But what about Jews? Now, Maya had sufficient Jewish ancestry to have a somewhat ambivalent attitude. And my godfather, Professor Alexander of Manchester, was a Jew (and of course I was an unbaptised bairn, so it was an oddish relationship, though a very satisfactory one) and he looked like an Old Testament prophet with his great brown beard and soft brown eyes. I was increasingly fond of him as I grew up and talked to him a lot about my literary ambitions, which he took seriously. By now I was going in for competitions in the pale green Saturday *Westminster*. Uncle Willie had given me a typewriter for my sixteenth birthday: a good little portable Corona which lasted me for years. In those days one got free lessons and I went to Hunt's in the Broad for them, but, though I have typed fairly fast for many years, I never use my fingers sufficiently and if I don't think I can see the keyboard, I don't touch-type properly. My father immediately asked me to type his papers, but was worried when I dropped a line, as one so easily does with copy typing; he felt I was not attending properly to the sense, nor was I. But how much better my own poems looked in type! I sent them sometimes to my godfather, who might afterwards discuss Beauty with me, to our mutual advantage. It was clear that being a Jew—that kind of Jew—was a proud and splendid thing. But many, alas, were not like him, as was made clear.

There was a friend or acquaintance of Jack's, most definitely a Jew and looking it. He was one of our frequent visitors for the parties where we played Nebuchadnezzar, and had acted in *Saunes Bairos*. Yes, there he is in the photograph. He was one of the 'natives'. I suspect that Maya thought he might be buzzing round me, though I rather doubt that this was so. At any rate she told me not to pick him if we were picking sides. I was often the picker, since the host and hostess were more likely to know everyone's names or nicknames—besides, I liked doing it! That evening the sides were picked, the known best actors and prettiest girls went first, then there was a smaller pool and at last, at the end, my pick and poor Clausen standing there—and was I to disobey Maya's explicit instructions? I certainly didn't dislike

84

him, but the prohibition had been given with great seriousness which I had not questioned. I still remember his darkish, injured face, his eyes dropped to the floor, suffering as Jews have suffered for a long time. There was some kind of rush, joke, compromise, diplomatic lying, I don't know now. I was confused, felt awful, not so much for him but for myself having been put into this position by some sort of net I didn't understand but which had caught us both, Clausen and me. Yet I didn't protest, I was too embarrassed to say anything further to my mother; there must have been some reason which I didn't grasp, so it was probably my fault. Occasionally, if I had lied my way out of a situation, I would have a word of praise for my social sense; this kind of lying was quite all right, and the parallel suppressions of truth. Nor do I know whether this poor young man came to any more Neb parties—this may well have been one of the last before, so to speak, the ceiling came down: before August 1914. Nor do I know if he was still there when we started picking up the pieces in 1918.

Anti-Semitism as such would definitely not have been approved. As far as colour went, Indian 'natives' were approved if in the Army or even as students if sufficiently high caste, polite and well connected. Maoris were definitely all right, perhaps because of their enthusiastic acceptance by Rob Makgill, our much loved cousin, chief M O of Auckland. Perhaps also Stevenson's poems and stories of Polynesia helped, though I doubt if I had ever seen anyone from those still delectable islands. But I am almost sure I never met any African socially, though as a child I had stared at the inhabitants of 'African villages' at shows. Chinese and Levantines were the picture-book villains, but the brave little Japs, who had so valiantly defeated the big Russians, were still admired.

As to religious barriers, we knew a few Roman Catholic families, but I think my mother was always slightly suspicious of those who gave allegiance to the 'Bishop of Rome'. And there was always a slight background of walling-up nuns, and, of course, of the lower-class Irish who were distinctly undesirable, even as servants. Our maids would normally attend some religious service on their Sundays off: Chapel was very suitable, but they might also be C of E. My mother would have been careful about food, not to break any known religious rules, either for Jews, Moslems or such Brahmins or Buddhists as might have been invited. This was standard social manners. I rather doubt whether these various fine lines and distinctions meant much to my father, though he was certainly a fairly stern moralist, taking a much more conventional attitude on such things than one might have expected.

But there was another strange race: men. I am not sure what, if any, explicit sex instruction any of us had. The boys who were leaving the Dragon School had an admonishment from the Skipper, which I tried vainly to overhear by hanging about under a window, from which I was promptly dislodged. I think it was on the general cold-baths-to-avoid-temptation, and keep-your-hands-out-of-your-pockets, line. But girls? It seems odd if Frances and I never discussed this, yet, if so, I can't remember. Perhaps here there is a real memory blank, a depth of embarrassment, into the bottom of which my fishing memory cannot reach, just as I have utterly forgotten the probably erotic stories I told myself. I doubt whether any of the information we got was very inaccurate, certainly not deliberately so. It was the continuous slanting.

For instance, my mother told me that if anyone proposed marriage (no other proposal would conceivably have been a possibility!) I must ask whether he had ever had anything to do with another woman and if he had I must refuse him. This was straight feminism of the period, an attack on the double standard for men and women, which was still, of course, socially accepted. I wish I could remember the wording: 'slept with' perhaps? Or simply 'had a mistress'? One knew that from the history books.

It was asking for trouble, especially on the assumption that the man was normally at least five years older than the girl he married. If he was still a virgin nearer thirty than twenty, then there was likely to be something wrong. There was at this time no respectable sex instruction or advice book for either sex. My poor Dick, just before our marriage, seems to have asked a few questions of the regimental doctor, who said in a hearty and reassuring way that he would get to know soon enough. Might things have gone better if he had acquired some earlier experience? Perhaps. My mother was clearly longing to have a cosy last-minute chat with me, but I brushed her off, convinced that anyone who knew as much as I did about guinea pigs had no need of further knowledge. The notions of either sex about the expectations and needs of the other, whether in courting or in intercourse, were minimal. There was only the social assumption, reinforced to some extent by religious or educational exhortation, that the young man and young woman 'kept themselves' for their future spouse. Is it better, if you are dying in the agony of modern warfare, to regret what you haven't had or, perhaps, what you have? There were plenty of virgin soldiers in 1914. There was also a generation of women now past retiring age who lost their men for whom they had kept themselves, and never replaced them. They were historically important in the development of education, health, politics, the arts and sciences. In the next war the sexes died more evenly.

Over this business of parallel virginity, I jumped at the feminism and the implicit possibility of getting the better of a man, but did not in the least grasp the dangers of sexual ignorance. But I did grasp that for a man to 'have a mistress' was a nasty, continental thing—look at all those French kings!—and in Britain only practised by the *nouveaux riches*, themselves appropriately described in French.

Some of the rules were quite simple. I knew, for instance, by the time I was sixteen that one must not get into, or be seen in, a hansom cab alone with a man, unless one's brother. Hansoms were delightful, hopping up into such a good position for the view, the closing of the clever doors, the quick clopping of the hoofs; one always hoped to be allowed one at a London station. It was only if we had a lot of luggage or were in a family party that we had to take a growler—the smelly old four-wheeler. But the runners, who in my very young days used to run alongside

87

to help with the luggage in return for a small tip were, thank goodness, extinct. Or did they still do it in the bad bits of the industrial belt, out of sight of London and Oxford?

There were other rules about possible danger spots, such as hansoms. Being alone was always perilous in the imaginary jungle. I suppose the mothers of the period all fussed about their virgin daughters, possessors of so desirable a property. Hence the chaperones, the rules, the exhortations. Hence trouble for males suspected of interest, unless they were 'desirable' and their intentions were honourable, in which case they would delicately consult their prospective parents-in-law. One was told vaguely of certain loathly but un-named diseases which could be picked up, one was told, from used towels or glasses and especially lavatory seats. Hence anyone visiting 'the continent' took a supply of paper lavatory seat covers. Did visitors from those parts do the same for England?

The virgin daughters tried to escape, but not too far. We were all somewhat scared; there was too much we didn't know. But our plans for the future always included more freedom. I was now vaguely thinking of architecture as a profession; I often used to scribble plans of houses, none, I think, of any merit, and I never could draw the outsides to look the way I wanted them to. However it was not yet possible for a girl student to become an architect in England, though it was in Scandinavia; so that was that. But what with guinea pigs, acting, reading, collecting wild flowers and day-dreaming, life was fairly full.

After a certain amount of parental agitation, it was decided that I could be allowed to 'come out', temporarily as I was firmly made to understand, in June 1914. It would be my brother's last Commem; my allowance was to be two Commem balls. In preparation for this there were several weeks of ball-room dancing classes at the Randolph. My partners were mostly in their last year at Oxford, or possibly in their second year. I suppose mixed ball-room dancing classes were something of an innovation—or weren't they? Were there Edinburgh dancing classes in the Assembly Rooms for bouncing Highland girls in for the season?

Mine were indeed a different matter from the old High School classes. What I enjoyed were the patterned dances with intricate steps, especially tangoing with Lewis. It was all building up towards the real thing. Jack and I did mostly heavy waltzes with little reversing, but seeing which of us could whirl longest without getting giddy. There were also delightful fast polkas. These classes were, naturally, ringed with chaperones; sometimes they ended in tea but often our partners had to rush back to College and work.

For the real thing I had a long white dress, silk georgette, I expect, with a fairly low neck, short sleeves and, to go with it, long white, pearl-buttoned kid gloves which took ages to get on. I wore it also for my first Old Dragon dinner, where I was the only female, among white-tied or black-tied white-fronted males. I was given a gold chain with a little opal drop in a blue enamel setting, my first 'real' jewellery, in preparation.

The real thing came, the carefully organised Commem parties, the instruction about behaviour, the photographs in the sleepy, bleary early morning. Not too much claret cup, come back between partners. See that you 'go into private life'—that was then the phrase—in good time, as there will be a queue. Above all, not too many dances with the same partner. But Mitch—was he yet Dick to me?—wandered down with me in my white dress to the empty High. A single motorbike came and went, passing Univ and Queen's and I saw for the first time, the shape, the exact, beautiful curve of the High, normally blotted by two-way traffic, but suddenly clear. We both saw it.

We girls were always rather thrilled at the news of an engagement. On the whole in our class, marriage was somewhat later than now, when the husband could be expected to provide for his wife in the manner to which she was accustomed. In the respectable or rising working class, it was often considerably later. Couples walked out for years on their half day off. And walking was probably about all they managed to do. Any of us in Miss Blockey's classroom would have reacted violently against being kissed, unless possibly a light and respectful touch on the brow. A flirtation did not necessarily involve any contact. There were no love scenes in my plays and they didn't even come in much in Nebs or charades, where we tended to have battles, murders or incidents where our fancies were free to embroider ('Alexander the coppersmith has wrought me much evil') or which could be used to puzzle an audience ('Is it M for Marat or A for Agamemnon in the hip bath, vigorously soaping himself?') or needed great ingenuity (Lord Burleigh 'walking up and pacing down', Enoch Arden's funeral, Cerberus with his three heads, Canute with the waves coming in). Today C (or K) for Circe would be seducing O (or U) for Odysseus; but then she was turning the crew into realistically grunting swine.

We usually cleared up the acting box ourselves, but otherwise tidying and washing-up was just left. In the morning it was done. One was unfamiliar with the process. Dusters, soap, soda? These belonged to another world. A trusted maid informed my mother of what was needed; no doubt she checked occasionally. There were locked store cupboards, as well as a strong-room and cellar. Once I was taken to a country house where there was a genuine still-room in which essences were made, interesting drinks and bunches of dried herbs, and there was an impressive and beautifully labelled and arranged array of jam, jelly, chutney and so forth. But this was not at all my mother's line; the early twentieth-century feminists had thrown all that off, though we did make a fair amount of jam. However jam-making was the cook's depart-ment, although the family did the picking, whether of wild or garden fruit, and servants' work ranked low. A kitchen maid cut her hand, which I did up with iodine, lint and bandages. Shortly afterwards I was discovered to have nits in my hair; probably the kitchen maid was given notice! Lice were very lower class; if anyone caught them it was extremely shameful, that is to say until World War One, when any kilted soldier, officer or private, coming back on leave, would almost certainly have to have a very hot iron run along the seams of his kilt.

These fine shades of class distinction are rather hard to get into perspective, and most of all my own acceptance of them. But there they were, and are still in societies which have sufficient spare time and energy to bother about them, that is to say in all the countries we know though they change and shift with the years! Class divisions today may be along lines of money or caste, party or religion. Whatever division it is, most people in the country concerned accept it as natural and obvious. I tend to feel divisions most clearly today along education lines, by which I don't mean qualifications, but the intellectual freedom and wide-ranging sets of knowledge which an educated person should have. And yet—and yet—there are other values, honour and courage and generosity, which used to be thought of as the virtues of gentle birth, but which are, as we should know by now, not the prerogative of any class or race.

Did I ever become educated? If so, only accidentally and occasionally, with a few questions filled in during odd times in the lab, or perhaps talking with distinguished guests. I suppose it was in late 1913 or early 1914 that I sat 'Locals' in some Oxford public building. I'm not sure what they corresponded to and have an idea that there were Junior and Senior, the latter being equivalent to university entrance. The standard, especially perhaps in science, was clearly much lower than today. I don't recollect being worried by these exams or even doing any hard work, in fact all I remember is a very easy Botany paper, with a specimen flower to dissect and label. It had two small green caterpillars inside it, which I made race across my desk.

IX

Inside Naomi Haldane

And what about the ghosts and devils or whatever they were? The appearances that beset me if I wasn't careful? Well, they were still around. And are, though not so obtrusively, and as one grows older one finds means of making them work for one, as in a number of episodes in *We Have Been Warned* and *The Bull Calves*. By fourteen I was no longer worried about treading on the lines between paving stones. Finials on the ends of North Oxford tile ridges ceased to look at me. But I was still very conscious of good and bad in houses and in furniture, especially mirrors. Our expeditions into curiosity shops in search of wedding presents might bring one suddenly face to face with something which was clearly hostile, a twister of the straight look. I noticed much the same, not many years back, in the Soane Museum, which I suppose I ought to re-visit. But probably won't.

I was also beginning, in my reading, to come across passages in which it was clear that the authors were describing and had experienced, my kind of thing: fairly often in Kipling short stories, occasionally in Wells, Eden Philpott or Buchan. The last time I remember being struck in the same kind of way was in the last chapter of *The Teachings of Don Juan*, a book which had interested me very much. I read this at Mochudi in Botswana, in 1972, by candlelight certainly, but in my friendly white-washed rondavel where I could normally feel nothing but goodness and safety. At the end of the book I took a tablet of librium, but had the father and mother of a nightmare, one of the old kind. Nor am I the only one to be affected by this book. I am only thankful it didn't come my way when I was a lot younger.

The older parts of Cloan were still frightening and there were bad patches even in the glen. Does one ever completely grow out of such things? Of course not. They are as much part of oneself as one's bones. The best one can do, perhaps, is to have convincing dreams in which one traverses the black spots but the expected evil does not emerge. Occasionally my father comes into such dreams as the area of safety, occasionally as the exorciser or perhaps the explainer who makes it quite clear that as a matter of fact and once one grasps the pattern of what it is all about, everything is perfectly all right. In these dreams I am often aware that my father is, actually, dead, but that seems to make it all the more probable that he can help. There is nothing to be afraid of. In these reassuring dreams it is always my father, never my mother, once the childhood dispenser of safety and reassurance, the one on whom one had become dependent. It seems hard that poor Maya, who always longed to protect me, should not be able to do so! It is also curious that it is my father, who in life could not realise my frantic horror of bogles, nor how the family teasing only drove me into deeper terrors, has now become my dream understander and sympathiser. To each his own unconscious.

The nightmares were bad during my teens, I would think once a week at least in the worst patches, and not helped by the economically low-powered electric lights which one must always be sure to turn off at the landings. But how well was I? Or any of us? It was taken for granted that one would from time to time during the winter months have a bad cold, an earache or a cough that went on and on. These were depressing, to say the least. So was the sense of guilt if one's bowels were not regular, especially if one had lied slightly about them. One took tonics, though at least no longer cod liver oil which was perhaps out of fashion, and inhaled Friar's Balsam. Later, in the thirties, when I used to get these winter coughs, heroin lozenges got rid of them, nor do I remember ever getting addicted—they were rather nasty. But cough lozenges were part of winter life, from the chemist next to Gee's, formamints said to contain formalin and if so surely rather bad for one, and of course the delicious blackcurrant Allen and Hanbury's, for which it was well worth simulating a cough. At some point some kind Australian sent my mother a box of eucalyptus lozenges. As a British Empire product these were specially welcomed and after that she often got whole packages of them; I liked them myself and even found them fairly effective. The routine yearly visits to the dentist were rather fun than not, for I had a good dental inheritance and had also been breast-fed. Of course no dentist was a gentleman and one could never meet one socially.

But, to return to the nightmares, there was something very peculiar and alarming about them, or rather about a condition which was not sleep or dreaming, since I was often perfectly conscious of the external world and sometimes even had my eyes open, though this was difficult, as my eyelids stiffened. In this state I was held, unable to move, while something rushed by or through me—through, it seemed when I could manage to concentrate, the base of my skull—apparently taking with it some part of my thinking or will. This was sometimes preceded by a tension, not quite pain, but a feeling of alarm and distress, equally in the base of the skull. Whether this had any connection with my early concussion, I don't know. But it seems possible that it was a very mild form of *petit mal*, something which probably affects far more people, especially children, than one might suppose. The condition still very occasionally occurs, but is not alarming as it used to be. One knows it will pass: 'they' will let go, not really being as powerful as all that; one will soon return to normal.

No doubt part of this general ill health was due to the remarkably unheated state of British houses. The copper and brass hearth around the drawing-room fire was nice to sit on, but one couldn't do that all the time. Draughts breathed round one's ears. And most grates had slow combustion devices which were economical both of fuel and heat. It was all coal at Oxford and a coal cellar holding perhaps five tons from which the polished coal scuttles were brought. When it was used up one rang for more and still there was always an under housemaid to bring it. Sometimes I or Jack brought in a log of wood but it was usually elm or willow, not much good for burning. At least at Cloan one could gather fir cones. But there again, the usual solution was to ring for more coal. There were the new electric bells, which were not as decorative as the old china bell handles, but doubtless as unwelcome in the kitchen, where it was clear which room had been ringing.

I doubt whether there were any electric fires yet. But there were hot water bottles in plenty. In the inner laboratory there was a gas fire, another in the main bathroom. I expect it had been installed for Granny, perhaps for her maid to heat something—it had a gas ring. But it was seldom lighted; we were all chary about gas. Indeed for me the word had already a sinister connotation to be brought into sharp focus with the Battle of Ypres.

Yet, although conditions of ill health probably made a good breeding ground for nightmares and obsessions, it was kept bottled up, under considerable pressure. When the intellect was involved, it did not show, nor during the happiness of communal activity—conversation, playing games, acting. Nothing could touch me during the times of aesthetic satisfaction. Only, the head would lift, suddenly. I could not have spoken to anyone about the ghosts. Nor, as yet, could I use them as raw material for writing. That would have been too like touching them or being touched by them. They could have revenged themselves. And yet the first time I was to use them, in a verse drama, *The Mirror and the Clock*, was only a few years on, might have been already incubating. But it would have been risky still to put them onto paper; instead I wrote endless bits of romantic verse, but at least it always scanned:

> Deep in the north, a silver flame,
> The pole star pointing whence we came.

It was impossible to speak of my under-life to anyone who would treat the whole affair on a rational basis. Indeed this is only too clearly what happens often enough to mental patients. They must be met half-way with understanding, as I am sure happens when there is a combination of good psychiatry with enough time. One can't be rushed when pulling out these thorns.

My brother had the irrational streak, but he would probably have thought it inappropriate to share it with me. I could not speak to him, still less to parents or teachers. It would never have entered my mind to speak to a doctor. I could not have mentioned such things to my classmates, who would either have laughed or thought less highly of me as a competitor or leader. I told Andrew Lang of the nice bits of the irrational world and may perhaps have mentioned that not all the appearances were pleasurable, but if so he did not notice but encouraged me to see fairies; this I did from time to time, the last encounter being on the way back from the 1937 Labour Party Conference at Brighton—we had stopped to eat sandwiches and talk about George Lansbury. I happened to notice a hobyah type of fairy just going away.

The first attack on the powers of evil came suddenly and without preparation. I was sixteen. Jack's Eton friend, Mitch, was coming on an evening picnic up the river; when the flotilla set out, he was in my canoe and we were sufficiently alone on the green-shadowed brown of the slow water. I don't remember how it started, but suddenly I was telling him everything about the clock and the chair, the claw-legged mirror, the nightmares, the deep currents of fear and propitiation, and he was responding, not with disbelief or rationalisation, but with understanding. With love, doubtless, though I did not think of it in that word. What I experienced was an extraordinary sense of relief. I had spoken. They had not got back at me, were not able to. I had touched them and no evil current had passed; another hand was holding mine. What I did not realise was that, in partial—at least—breaking of a relationship between myself and my nightmares, I had inevitably started an equally deep counter-relationship between myself and Mitch, and that this relationship would key in with Rouen Cathedral, the tension and the delight.

But before that, in my mid-teens, when it would have been normal, why did I never become religious in any formal sense? Might not that have been effective anti-nightmare stuff? Well,

PROGRAMME.

Extra = Hossie

1 VALSE ...*Gielgud*...........
2 TWO-STEP..*Aldous*...........
3 BOSTON..*Dick*.................
4 LANCERS .*Austin*...........
5 ONE-STEP.*Morres Campbell*
6 VALSE *Leonard*...............
7 TANGO*..*Somerville Smith*
8 REEL...*R. Cross*.............

Hossie
Aldous
9 VALSE ...*Boswell*...........
10 MILITARY TWO-STEP.*Martin*.
11 SWEDISH DANCE ..*Leonard*..
12 BOSTON..*Stallery*...........
13 ONE-STEP...*and!*.............
14 VALSE ....*Dick*.............
15 SIR ROGER DE COVERLEY
     AND GALLOP....*Boy*......

* You may boston.

CHERWELL, *1st extra = Dirley*
Nov. 7, 1913. *2nd " = Hossie*

Our last joint birthday party before the War.
My dance programme

I am showing off my engagement ring in this photograph from 1914.
Me, Dick, J. D. Walker, an old friend from Dragon
School days, and Jack

I suppose I was just not that kind of person. Perhaps magic and religion don't entirely mix; I have never quite appreciated what, to others, seems a clear boundary line. I certainly made some attempts to acquire a rational Haldane-type *weltanschaung*. I began trying to read Hegel. That sentence, however, might have been written about any decade of my life up to the sixties when instead it might have changed to: I stopped trying to read Hegel. But he did seem to be part of the family tradition. There was enjoyable old Plato, with the settings of the dialogues, but I was uninterested in the genuine philosophy. I pushed myself, or was pushed, through Berkeley and even parts of Hume, though now I think of Hume, not as a philosopher, but as one of the Edinburgh eccentrics. But Christianity, as exemplified either in New College chapel or in either of the Auchterarder Free Churches, had no impact. One just couldn't take things like the Creed seriously, as they stood. Later I was more inclined to allow for the historical context, to admit that, in a sense, there might be validity in some of the statements. If by any chance I now find myself at a Church of England service, I tend to repeat the General Confession. One may as well keep oneself reminded of the things one has done or left undone.

But other religions, or hierarchies, were more attractive, although what one felt was not belief, whatever that is. In different adolescent moods, Apollo, Artemis, Dionysos, or even the grey-eyed Athene, found a temporary votary. I still thought highly of the Norse pantheon, fed by versions of sagas. And I was beginning to involve myself with the Celts, first through *Celtic Fairy Tales*, then through Lady Gregory's *Gods and Fighting Men*. And there was a book about Isis and Osiris which I much enjoyed. At Cloan I varied my old gardens for fairies by building altars to unknown gods and making offerings of flowers and berries and small scarlet toadstools, sometimes in a pleasingly pre-Constance Spry manner.

Then of course there were all those fascinating Swinburnian deities, Cotytto, Astarte and Astaroth—'in Lampsacus fervent with faces, in Aphaca red from thy reign,' which places I even looked up in Murray's classical maps. But when, with the aid of the *Encyclopaedia Britannica*, one tried to find out a bit more about these deities, they turned out to be rather horrid. I suppose I read all Gilbert Murray's translations of Greek plays, and was of course much interested in the Furies whom I recognised; and there was the occasional Greek play in the Summer Term. It was Jack's friend, Mitch again, who tried to lure me into learning Greek with a charming little book: *Lalage ou le Grec sans Larmes*, but that didn't take. He did however give me a lovely edition of Leconte de l'Isle, whose high-tragedy Norse mythology appealed to me enormously. My own stories at the time were full of heroic deaths, since this was not the hideously common thing it was to become not so far ahead. The book was exquisitely bound in red morocco with my initials on it in a small gold motif. We went together to the binder's workshop in Long Wall Street, up a flight of wooden steps, close under the old City wall, the other side from New College garden.

But the religion that really got a grip on me was Mithraism. One attractive aspect of this was that I always imagined myself a man, a friend no doubt of Pertinax and Parnesius in Kipling's version of the Wall, or else one of the equally Kiplingish Winged Hats, in which case the Norse side of things could slide in happily. I read Mithraism up in some detail when I was writing *Prisoners of War*; the reference books included Cumont's *Mystères de Mithra*; at least I was able to read French easily by now. There was a Buchan story too that gripped me. Then came those July plays and the wreathed altar and my hair bunched up into what was supposed to be a Greek fillet. And Mitch (but now, surely, he was Dick) wrote:

> The gods, O faithful mystic, are not dead.
> They wheel and murmur through the summer night,
> And shaping dimly round thy lifted head
> They come once more into the waning light
> And lead again such dances as they led
> Through Thessaly, in swift enraptured flight.
> The Gods, O faithful mystic, are not dead.'

Oh many were they, far and wide their praises
Once sounded. Last of all, from tower to tower,
Even far Solway saw the upturned faces
Turned towards Mithras at the evening hour.
Where now, save on this hill, are their high places,
Where now, save here, are heard the words of power?
The Gods, O faithful mystic, are not dead.

After that the probable next step should have been clear to me. But was not. Yet I had already written a poem myself about the New College Commem ball, which should have informed me about myself and my dance partner, with whom I was sitting out. Again it did not. But it is an almost grown-up poem.

Sitting Out

The Chinese lanterns in broad day
Like orange ghosts show faint and strange,
We feel the throb of dancing feet,
The distant music's halt and change;

I thought I heard,—did you not hear?—
Piercing the golden violins,
A foreman's whistle, sharp and clear:
They go to work; did you not hear?

The dancers stream across the grass,
The morning wind lifts up their hair;
The music deadens heart and brain,
They do not know, they would not care.

Surely you heard, as we sat here—
It pierced right through the violins—
That foreman's whistle, shrill and clear?
They go to work; and we sit here.

We should not come outside and flaunt
Bare necks and shoulders to the sun,
Our dresses look so hot and crushed,
We should have gone when night was done.

A moment since—too near, too near—
It pierced the singing violins,
That foreman's whistle, fierce and clear!
They go to work; with us so near.

X

The Sky Falls

In early August there was the Curragh incident. My mother
thought all the time about Ulster; nothing else seemed to matter.
Then in three days we were at war. A letter from one of the
cousins in California to my mother: 'You wrote two days before
it came and your fears were all of the Ulster troubles and then it
came in a moment.'

We would win, of course—we always did, didn't we? It was
wonderfully exciting; one wanted to rush around all the time.
For some reason we rushed to London and at my uncle's Queen
Anne's Gate house I saw Sir Edward Grey, the Foreign Secretary,
looking desperately anxious and worried. Wasn't it all going right?
It must be! Yet this was the first tiny doubt, a white-faced,
middle-aged man slowly shutting a door behind him, not noticing
a girl on the stair. Everything was disorganised. Our friends were
hurrying into khaki; many of the young men had been in OTC's
and now the way was open to real war—if only they could get out
soon before it was all over. It couldn't last until 1915! If anyone
seemed to hesitate, the girls—the older people as well—were
ready to push them into glory. Dick, who had left Oxford after his
expected First in Greats, was reading for the Bar and had joined
the Inns of Court OTC, a mounted body—he liked riding—and
from there was sent as a Second Lieutenant to the Queen's Bays
and a more severe riding school. Bey Gillespie, who had shared
the London flat, went off too, both of them leaving everything
just as it was—surely they'd be back soon! If only the war didn't
end without giving them a chance! So it seemed at first. My

brother had of course gone to the family regiment, the Black Watch, with his cousins.

Glory. Yes, it did honestly seem like that to me at sixteen. I was upset because I was 'out of the fun', as I might have put it. Or my mother might have, at first. We had Red Cross first aid and home nursing classes at Cherwell taught by a couple of nurses. At last I learnt how to make a bed. Frances and I bandaged one another, those splendid elaborate bandages that in practice one never used (except perhaps the capeline to keep a dressing on a very scabby head!) We found it rather exciting to see one another relatively unclothed. There were the songs: *Mademoiselle from Armentières*: *Tipperary* of course. Bernard Partridge drawing villainous Kaisers in *Punch*. Gallant little Belgium, the horror stories—babies tossed on bayonets, rapes spoken of in horrified whispers; eagerly we believed it all. The thing which really upset our household was the wrecking of pithead machinery at a working Belgian colliery, including of course the cage and ventilation. Yet most of it seems very mild compared with what we are used to now in any war and speak about aloud, see on television and then forget.

Then the casualties began. Inexplicably we were not winning and our friends began to be killed: really killed so that we would never see them again. Then it was clear the war was not going to be over by Christmas and all the men in training were threatened. We began to be afraid. Jack with the Third Battalion of the Black Watch up at Nigg was fairly immediately threatened as casualties came in from the First and Second Battalions. Pat, our first cousin, also in the Black Watch, was killed. Graeme, his brother, was in the Navy, off having adventures in the Mediterranean. Elsie became a nurse.

Meanwhile I had been asked down to Frolbury Manor, to stay with the Mitchisons. I did not at all realise that the respective mothers (at least) had spoken to one another or that I had been invited for a purpose. I think this was the first rail journey I had done quite by myself. Perhaps I was met at Paddington and driven down to Surrey; they had a big comfortable car with a chauffeur and carriage rugs. Probably I wouldn't have managed a change of stations in London. Everybody was very nice to me, nice to me myself, not just to the family. Yes, I was counted as a real person! I was fascinated with the comparative luxe of the house—the furnishings, the food, the china, my future mother-in-law's French maid, the fact that a bathroom opened out of my bedroom, a bathroom all bright and gleaming, better than Cloan, with stuff in bottles that I sniffed but didn't risk. Then Mitch—who now must be Dick—turned up in an incredibly smart cavalry uniform. I am inclined to think now that I might have said yes to the first man (I beg your pardon: officer) in uniform who asked me to marry him in August 1914. It would have been 'war work'; it would have been involvement in the great excitement. Anyway, it was Dick who did ask me.

I was extremely worried almost immediately afterwards at what I had done. I think this is, or was, fairly normal for a quite young girl who has accepted almost without thinking. And at that period an engagement was not something one could honourably get out of. Marriage—what was it really? Something gone for ever, all one's life changed. I had swapped the slight measure of freedom I was beginning to experience for—what? I felt that yet another set of grown-ups was going to own me. Even the shining bathroom was no longer fun. For the first time in my life I couldn't sleep.

I rushed back to Oxford so as to be in time for the first aid and home nursing exam, though this must have seemed a bit odd to the Mitchisons who wanted me to stay on. I took a cab from the station, dashed in, said to Maya, 'I'm engaged to Dick. Where's the exam going on?' and left her sitting in an understandably emotional state on the hall settee, vainly trying to ask questions. So that was that. I got my Red Cross certificate all right but I gave one wrong answer in the oral exam—peritonitis for peritoneum—why remember that for sixty years? I was told I mustn't say anything, even to Frances (whom I had already told, so there was a first bit of guilt complex) until there had been further consultations. It must have been soon after that Dick came to see my father, vainly trying to interest him in the financial details which his parents had told him to explain. Finally, asked about his interests, he said he was now reading the *Encyclopaedia Britannica*. 'Yes,' said my father, 'but do you understand it?' Poor Dick.

Jack seemed pleased when he heard. It was a deep and lifelong friendship not interrupted later on by little things like Dick being in the Labour Party and Jack in the Communist Party: of course Jack would come and speak for him! It was not interrupted by Jack's bitter quarrels with me; they went on swapping jokes and stories and information whenever they saw one another. Almost half a century after 1914 they were joking about one another's false teeth.

Nigg, where the Third Battalion had their camp, was a strange gaunt place. We stayed at a small farm with a most charming Highland family. Jack was now deep in this new life, intent on doing it as well as possible. Here he succeeded. A year or two later privates joining up in the Black Watch heard of Jock Haldane already as a story, a myth figure, a killer silently getting to the enormously dangerous but only correct spot from which to lob his bombs, often his own make, into the enemy trench and watch the shower of corpses. But he was also an officer to be completely trusted; his fatherly care of his men had taken them safe through utmost perils.

All the young men whom we had known in the old days developed an immense conscientiousness, perhaps some aspect of a shield against the kind of war which they were now beginning to be aware must be faced, however excitedly they had gone in at the start. Perhaps too something to set them apart from the civilian world where 'business as usual' was still going on. That was to become increasingly shocking to those with other standards and who were not profiting by it. Dick learnt an immense amount about the possible diseases of horses. The Queen's Bays were still practising cavalry charges. He was becoming aware that this was silly and wanted to change, but that was not easy.

I went down to Frolbury fairly often after this, at weekends.

Surrey was not yet a stockbroker's paradise, but partly at least a refuge for the intelligentsia, sometimes with cottages in genuine villages inhabited in the main by genuine villagers. It was a new botanical area for me, the sparse heathlands of dry Surrey, the smell of pines rather different from that in Scotland. We went walking in the woods, first in full summer then turning to autumn, winter with crunching beech leaves and at last spring. We met various interesting people, mostly left-wingers of some kind, including Amber Reeves, heroine of a much publicised affair with H. G. Wells. This shocked my mother deeply and I believe she protested about her innocent daughter meeting a 'loose woman', someone about whom there had been a major scandal. I doubt if it shocked Dick's mother; she, I am sure, was much more shocked by my lack of fashion sense—or even presentable clothes —and my social ungrown-upness as it appeared in her milieu, terrifying Aunt Kate and gentle Aunt Helen. I in turn found her sisters alarming and disapproving. She gave me a black velvet suit, a creamy *crêpe-de-chine* blouse with round blobs of buttons and a hat with a black cockade on the side. I didn't mind dressing up, but nobody was going to get me out of my clodhopping 'sensible' shoes into high heels, nor would I take any extra trouble over doing my hair in a more attractive way. I must have been singularly irritating.

Frolbury Manor was a largish modern country house, the main rooms looking south and opening on to a broad stone terrace with geraniums in tubs and garden chairs. Inside there was a big hall with sofas and rugs, overhung by a gallery. I doubt if it had any right to call itself a manor but it had a large garden, terraced down to a couple of paddocks with a stream winding through them and a small wood where we tried to make a swimming pool. There must have been several gardeners as well as a very complete household staff, and the big light drawing-room with its valuable furniture, pictures and china had always two or three banks of greenhouse flowers, brought in and arranged by the gardeners; I was much impressed, especially by the schizanthus which I had never met before. In one corner was a rather horrid large white Dresden china monkey, which later on always wore a captured *pickelhaube*; perhaps Willie put it there as a joke and nobody had the heart to to take it off. There were also splendid greenhouse carnations which were new to me, and gorgeous to put in one's hair, real dressing-up material, heavily clove-scented. At this point I had myself never used perfume or for that matter any other beauty aids. I would have found it shocking to do so. There was a billiards-room at Frolbury where Dick and I were supposed to conduct our courtship. As to that I was still unsure of anything. I couldn't explain that there were words and touches I didn't want. It had been somewhat of a shock to find that someone whom I had considered as another brother, somebody who had understood about the nightmares and not laughed, had suddenly turned into something else. Perhaps if it had been possible to take the whole thing at a slower tempo I would have been able to respond. But there was a war on and nothing could wait.

Dick did not get to France until the early summer of 1915. I went quite often to Frolbury and must have written to Gran-niema about it, when sending her a pin-cushion for her birthday— it is difficult to think of suitable presents for a ninety-year-old grandmother. She writes on April 10 1915, 'I do not exactly know the country, but I know something of the adjoining country, having seen a considerable part of it while driving in different directions. It is a very attractive part of England, and abounded with wild flowers, especially white violets to which I am much attached!'

I must have found and sent her some, no doubt well packed with moss, for the next letter, on April 19, says: 'I was very much pleased with the white violets. I am very partial to them and they remind me of Hampshire and Surrey and pleasant days there. I have some white Devonshire violets, but they are different and also some from Innerpeffray, but they are not in flower yet. They are in my garden and have a character of their own; I think they must have been there when the old Abbey was in use.' She writes too of Pat and of Jack, and of Graeme guarding convoys between Egypt and Asia Minor in the *Doris*. The wild flowers down south must have been a fortnight ahead of the Ochills, and with these subtle differences which, to the close looker, as Granniema and I both have been, are half the fun.

But, to go back to 1915, there is plenty more I remember about these months before Dick went off to France to join the Queen's Bays there, but it is not relevant. However, to show the completely different ambience of the times, here are two episodes from one of his 1915 leaves. Dick really enjoyed taking me out to meals; I was young and greedy with the digestion of an ostrich. To eat as many Fuller's cream cakes as I really wanted was heaven! But once he took me out to lunch at Simpson's. It was the first time I had ever had lunch in that kind of restaurant and I enjoyed it immensely. But our respective mothers got together and spoke to us very seriously indeed about how Dick's actions might have 'compromised' me. We were both very angry and upset; I wrote a bad and furious poem, but what was the use against grown-ups? Then, one leave, Dick was to come up with me to Cloan, meet Granniema and the family who all liked him—but we were not allowed to have sleepers (even first class, obligatory for him as an officer) on the same train. Again this would 'compromise' me. Remember we were formally engaged with an announcement in *The Times*. Nor was I at seventeen all that much of a shrinking violet. Anyhow that was the parental attitude, presumably that of millions of other upper-middle-class parents.

Twice in late 1914 my parents and I went up to Nigg by the Highland Line beyond Perth. Jack and I swam in the October North Sea, I decently turning my back and putting on a swimsuit. Did he? In those days no kilted regiment wore anything below the kilt except possibly for regimental full dress. I remember the rocks and the waves and later in the evening watching the full moon racing among the clouds, trying to take omens, for him of course. Apart from this I never swam for pleasure during the whole war. I wanted to of course in summer, but it seemed—well, I might have said unpatriotic, but it was even more irrational than that: if I could make a sacrifice perhaps the wrath would be averted from someone 'out there'. We went as a family to

Southampton to see Jack off with the Third Battalion, my parents putting on brave faces, I in terror that this was a final goodbye. It must have been very trying for him.

I remember with such embarrassment and distaste that my memory shies away, how my mother seemed determined to share all emotional passages with me. It was as though Dick's presence stirred her in a way that it did not stir me. He was certainly very fond of her and always very nice to her, but that was not at all the same thing. It was all mixed up with the war tension, the fact that now her God was threatened, the Empire itself, and these young men were the priests and/or the sacrifice. Curious how the sacrifice idea went deep in the family. Was it the Jewish streak from my mother's mother's side? It was quite different from the parallel but sensible idea that one must be prepared to take all risks, including that of one's life, for objectives that appear morally and intellectually sufficiently important. I also remember very clearly being told that the period of her engagement was the happiest time in a girl's life. This seemed to me to bode ill for marriage.

Then there was the problem of an engagement ring. Dick gave me a family ring, Australian gold in small knobs run together into a circle. It was a little too big for me and one day I had taken my mother's invalid cousin Archie up the river punting. Wet from the punt pole, the ring slipped off my finger. I dived for it without even taking my shoes off, grovelled in the mud bottom of the Cherwell, but failed to get it. Dick was immensely sweet and comforting about it, I mustn't take it as an omen—what other ring would I like? I didn't like to say that what I really wanted was a star sapphire, just by itself, no diamonds. I did mutter something about blue stones. His mother went to an antique shop in Brighton and sent several rings for me to choose. The only blue one was turquoise which I didn't like. I chose one with small emeralds and diamonds, which I never liked as much as the gold one; Dick and I agreed to sell it later on to buy something for the house. But his parents also gave me a double string of small pearls, with a diamond and emerald clasp which later I turned into

108

something else. It was an almost overwhelming present. My future mother-in-law wore coloured pearls, pink and grey, large, and I would think very valuable. But I never quite saw the point of them.

The only other one of the family whom I was really fond of was Dick's younger brother Willie. He had volunteered as a despatch rider; he was a dear, gay and affectionate, with a certain talent for drawing. He got a Blighty early on and a few months in hospital and on leave, but unfortunately it was too mild a wound. He was killed in 1916. I don't think his parents ever really recovered.

XI

The Impact

Oxford in wartime still managed a certain amount of gaiety. But the colleges were emptying; Aldous Huxley came and stayed with us, which was nice. Now that Miss Blockey was away he played for my dancing and he asked me what being in love was like. But I, not being 'in love', did not answer satisfactorily. At first he was badly depressed though not speaking much about Trev, but gradually he began to unshell. There were things happening, a few poets left, the university co-op shop which we took turns to staff—this was great fun, almost like acting. I loved being behind the counter. That, rather than the political side of the co-operative movement, was the attraction. In the room above I experienced my first grown-up style committees. There was a co-operative dressmaker who made Earp, one of our poets, some pyjamas out of a piece of Liberty silk he had bought; they had the word 'Liberty' on the selvedge and this was incorporated in the trouser legs. How we laughed!

I was beginning cautiously to investigate politics, or rather to see the man who interested Agnes Murray so much, for I loved Agnes, Gilbert Murray's beautiful daughter—our families were by now on friendly terms—and she admired G. D. H. Cole, the dark and flashing Magdalen revolutionary. Or so he appeared to young sillies like me. I doubt if he ever spoke to me at this time, but that didn't matter. I was allowed to go, so long as the meetings did not go on too late. I went to several where guild socialism was discussed; I didn't understand, but liked the taste of it all.

Meanwhile I managed to absorb a fair amount of learning; for me lectures had a certain interest but dissection had much more, especially the elegant inside of a pithed frog. Worms were all right but the crayfish tended to disintegrate and the dogfish were foul. The rabbit was interesting but I didn't care for its dead face. Guessing slides was fun too and the lab technicians, I think, went out of their way to help Dr Haldane's young daughter. It was no part of that year's course, but I also went to some more advanced lectures on genetics. But I never got on well with physics and chemistry; one of the lecturers tried to kiss me, which I didn't like at all, yet probably giggled while dodging, which only led him on. One simply couldn't help this giggling and it often had quite unintended results.

I was what was then called a Home Student, though now we are St Anne's and have a very attractive College of our own and a high academic standard. But at that date there was a rather limited academic supervision. I remember nothing in the nature of a tutorial system. There was just tea with the Principal in one of those monumental houses in Parks Road. It was perhaps rather unfortunate that she was more interested in educating her girls than in getting them degrees. Perhaps those of us with academic homes were supposed to be looked after already. Women's higher education was still rather new and unorganised. I doubt whether Somerville, where I would have liked to go, would have taken a sixteen-year-old, as I was at the beginning of the academic year in autumn 1914. Somerville and Lady Margaret Hall were the only women's colleges which had really made strong and permanent growth by that time, though the others were beginning, sometimes in rather temporary buildings.

We did botany in spring in the old botany labs facing out across the botanical gardens, a lovely place. I learnt to cut sections of plant material with an old cut-throat razor that my father had given me; I learnt to stain and the elements of microscopy. It was more than half a century afterwards that I used again the techniques I learned then, at Mochudi with the microscope I brought to the school; they were still in my head and fingers. Professor Vines was our lecturer and I remember that the life cycle of ferns had just been discovered; I don't think we got as far as fungi or lichens. But plant cells are large and beautiful and convincing, stomata are easy to see; botanical drawing is a pleasure; and we could take our lunchtime sandwiches out into the gardens or down on the close-mown green grass by the river.

It was only when men came back on leave or wounded that we imagined at all accurately what the fighting was really like—so far from Oxford and ourselves. But could we really imagine it as it was? No. In the papers news was edited and censored; it always is in wartime but we were not yet used to automatic disbelief of the kind that is usual now. We kept on thinking that it must be over soon. Then came the first gas attacks, my father hurrying out to headquarters in France where Jack joined him, the post mortem on the Canadian officer, the certainty that it was chlorine, the experiments to get an efficient gas mask, then coming back across the Channel to find Kitchener appealing to the women of England to make a totally useless mask which would only betray the men it went to. My father describes this at length in his own papers and one gets a sense of his anger and frustration. But his own lab was mobilised; all the men who were still there were completely involved in the struggle to make a cheap and efficient gas mask. The house reeked of chlorine, the noise of coughing and retching was continuous from the study and beyond. Everything that would make into a mask was seized on—stockings, vests, Aldous' woolly scarf, my knitted cap. They got it right in the end and then there was violent telephoning to the War Office. Aldous did most of the necessary type-writing. I remember my father, cut off, shouting at the operator: 'Damn you, I'm the Lord Chancellor!'

More wrong gas masks, but at last the right ones getting made and going out, though exasperatingly slowly. The women of England ones never left London; that had simply been a ploy to ease civilian tension and fear. But I had been sent round to stop our neighbours making them, urging them to wait till the right design came out—every mother wanted to send a gas mask to her own boy. I felt even then that some of the neighbours were suspicious and probably felt that these Haldanes were pro-

Dick in 1915

My father

German after all. Later my father was not put on to the committee on gas warfare, just because his brother had been attacked by the Harmsworth Press for a few remarks about German philosophy and for having been at a German university. That may well have resulted in a few extra deaths of men in the British Army.

If my brother had not been sent for to headquarters to work on the gas he would almost certainly have been in the fatal charge at Richebourg L'Avoué where most of the officers of the Third Battalion of the Black Watch were killed. He got to the front in time to see it happening far off, was himself wounded behind the front line by a shellburst, then picked up and taken to a field dressing station by the Prince of Wales, who was trying, as he always did, to get as near as possible to the real fighting and danger. Jack came home with a useful Blighty which kept him with us for weeks. How marvellous to have him back! What fun we had! But the caked dirt and lice on his kilt, that was something real too.

By that time I had managed to make various other girl friends, mostly my fellow Home Students. Some were Catholics staying at their hostel, Cherwell Edge. Was it then I got to know Liz Belloc, whose life so twined with mine later on? How nice it was for everyone when they had a young man to go around with again, especially perhaps one who had been wounded and was therefore approved of by the authorities. Many of my fellow Home Students were the daughters of Oxford parents. We were kept within the family bounds. I still of course had to be home for dinner and in bed at 'a reasonable hour', probably ten. I still slept in my mother's room. I was still afraid of the hall clock and dodged the clawed mirror.

Smoking was, of course, as immoral as reading forbidden books. I did however do both, but I really rather disliked smoking, just as I found *Madame Bovary* vastly dull, not worth struggling through in French. So, having made my point, to myself and, doubtless, to Frances and Aldous, I didn't persevere. Not liking tobacco smoke was a great nuisance later on in the twenties when any party, and above all any meeting, was thick and stinging with smoke from the addicts.

We Home Students had a common room in Ship Street whose amenities I enjoyed enormously. I could feel, once I was inside, that I had really got away from home. We could have coffee—by that time I had begun to like it—and buns or cakes which were still plentiful in 1915. There was a decent little loo where, in 1916, I had one of these very early miscarriages which are so usual; I told nobody. I must have had a slightly larger allowance by that time, but still can't have done any serious shopping unless possibly for a pencil or for yet another packet of hair pins. We weren't allowed to have men in—but a wounded officer on leave and a Haldane at that—well, when he dived under the sofa, whichever female don it was who came in pretended not to see. To conform with the rules, Helen Simpson, a keen rider, attached a lump of sugar to the end of her riding crop and dangled it out of the window for Jack to jump for. I expect we were scolded, but not hard. Much was allowed to Our Boys.

Aldous meanwhile had discovered Garsington, the house where Lady Ottoline Morrell held court and was hostess to so many distinguished or promising officers. How exciting it sounded! But alas, I was never allowed to go there. Frances did; she was less firmly kept in bounds than I was. Her grandfather was dead, so they were no longer in Wadham; they had a house halfway up Boar's Hill with a big garden where she and I used to play—and I have a feeling that we were still playing make-believe games. But I think she felt shy at Garsington; like so many highbrow paradises then and since it was more a place for young men than young women. I resented being kept out of it even if it harboured people of doubtful morals and conscientious objectors, surely the lowest of the low.

It was part of a world of minor arts which seemed marvellous at the time just because they were a break from the first decade of the century. There were also numbers of japes and harmless practical jokes. Aldous writes to me about one of them:

'Next Sat there is to be a conciliabule at the Co-op of Patricians—or members of a non-existent St Patrick's Club. There will be tea where you'll meet Robin ffaussett, Grattan Esmonde, myself and the Inimitable Miss Cox—together with others—including supers such as parsons, buffons, old ladies to act as chaperones. It will be funny, so come. You can be one of the non-Irish members like myself—the joke being that the tame parson thinks it's a serious meeting for the spread of Urse and Keltic Kultur!... I am frightfully busy, having to write an essay and a vast literary paper by Monday and Tuesday respectively—neither of which I've touched so far. But—will you come to tea on Wed—not unaccompanied by your mother, if she'd care to ...'

I don't think I can have managed to get to this, for how could I have forgotten something which was such fun? And mild enough compared with today's more bloodthirsty and violent jokes.

He writes again about my wedding:

'How admirable! I shall be on the spot all right, I think. Pity it's not to be ecclesiastical—I would have made such an excellent Page. Meanwhile what in the nature of a wedding present do you want? Unless you tell me I shall get something jolly like a set of real old Victorian antimacassars. I saw Gervas yesterday in quite good form.'

And a PS 'Did Frances get through her exams?'

And finally as the wedding day came nearer:

'Should you care to commit your last indiscretion before you become a British Expeditionary Force Matron by coming to tea on Wednesday? I am asking Frances to come. I trust the IMPURE PURPLE picture may by then have arrived.'

What he finally gave me was a somewhat Art Nouveau print of a veiled figure, yes, purplish. I was delighted with it then but in some of our moves or other troubles it disappeared.

These are cheerful letters and his gaiety and affection show even in the handwriting which is not that of a depressed or anxious person. It doesn't hurt to re-read them as it hurts to read the letters of those who were going to be killed. Aldous lived and left a life's work clearly stated at the end. In the gaps between slaughters we were being teenagers with our own delights and problems, our embarrassments and importances and giggles and glimpses of overwhelming beauty and excitement.

In the middle of all this I managed to get through science prelims. It was hot June weather and the slides dried up. The crayfish were disintegrating so that it hardly mattered where one stuck in the green gland flag label. I had been reading around a bit and brought in some remarks out of an early Julian Huxley, perhaps his first, at some point in my written paper. I thought, and rightly, that the examiner would not have read this book and would not have recognised the quotations as being anything except my own intelligence. The viva was all right except that when the examiner took a dog's skull out of a paper bag I was nearly overwhelmed with giggles because it looked as if it was going to be sandwiches. However, I kept my cool and remembered the foramina. I got through. I sometimes wonder if this was not because the examiners didn't have the face to turn down a young Haldane.

XII

The Letters

In come all the ghosts, including my own. But I got by and went on into another life with other values and a different set of words. So did Dick. So did Jack. But so many of the rest—no. And here are the letters, anything from privates to major-generals. Most are very young officers recently commissioned and apparently, in spite of their higher and expensive education, swallowing whole in the autumn of 1914 what was a very primitive form of patriotism, fuelled by newspaper propaganda, and using the kind of phrases which today make one shudder, since one has become aware of the realities and motives underneath them. It was as though these curiously innocent young men were utterly uncritical of anything their elders told them. Criticism—disbelief of any kind—was unpatriotic. This makes for a terrible embarrassment and sadness, re-reading these letters, which are all round me where I have undone the bundles or looked into the heavy manila envelopes that wait for me like hungry bivalves in a coral reef. Rupert Brooke said it for us; his war poems are hard to take now although then they were just what we thought we wanted. I find myself overwhelmed by pity and anger. It is particularly hard to find Dick, with his normally incisive mind, using these dreadful phrases, though perhaps rather more in letters to my mother than me. After all, mothers-in-law must be placated and perhaps he thought me too young for these big ideas of country and sacrifice.

The letters to my mother are sometimes from older people, using the set phrases which all the same came naturally. 'We Canadian mothers are so proud of our sons being permitted to take part in the great struggle of our Mother Country.' Or again from an old soldier to whom my mother had given money and a pair of old boots so that he could walk back to his regiment: 'Now i shall have a Chance to go out to the Front and do my Duty once again for my Country and help my chums out their.'

The letters are flimsy, often written in pencil with the red stamp giving no date or place and the corner saying 'Passed by Censor'. This letter written in the summer of 1914 was from someone to whom my mother had clearly sent a parcel. We were always doing them up and sending them off. He says, 'The iodine tincture was a particularly happy thought for my own had been lost.' It looks as though people had to make up their own first aid packets. It goes on:

'You will be glad to know we had a lively time the first night we spent in the trenches. The Germans entertained us to everything but gas. We had been sent in for instruction and were attached to an infantry battalion. We had such a doing we never expected to see the morning. In the company to which I was attached one officer was killed, one wounded, so it fell to my duty to take over two platoons and my own troop and to reorganise the defence.

'The OC of the company was kind enough to thank me for my assistance and man enough to say he did not know what he would have done without the extra men.

'I can't tell you how proud I am of my troop. It may sound extravagant but I love them all for every man was a fighter. The apparent wash-out is one of the surprises: my weediest trooper, when hit, had his wound bound up and stuck to the parapet till dawn, refusing to quit his post while there was any danger.'

There are letters of pure grief. This from Dick in October 1915, from Flanders. The evening before

'We'd had the Maire and the schoolmaster to dinner and I got so utterly exhausted talking French to them . . . Nou, isn't it

cruel about Heath? I heard from your Mother yesterday. Chug*
and then Gillie and then that wonderful little man, one after
another. There's no use in whining about it—but it did hurt,
didn't it? And does still—half the magic gone out of things.
And I do remember so many, many times spent with him.
He'll be the most mourned of them all; he did so much for
everyone. They're all such empty words for something so rare
that's gone—it's horrible to write about it. Writing about it calls
up all the times I've been up there, in that room, and all the
things we did and said.'

He goes on: 'Our winter billets will be just S.W. of —' And here
the censor has scratched out a name in purple pencil which spreads
more or less over the whole letter. Like tears. Does one wonder
that the first years of peace after that war were singularly desolate
for the young survivors?
And now here is one from Major-General Egerton in command
of the 52nd Lowland Division, written from Gallipoli in August
1915. I quote this fairly fully as it seems to be a bit of history.

'From the English papers it is clear that you know nothing
and hear very little and are told very little of what goes on
here. Possibly, indeed probably, it is necessary for Army reasons.
All I can say is that when I think of Winston's statement "that
we are only separated by a few miles from the greatest victory
the world has ever seen" I wish I had him out here.
'We can hold our own here, we can occasionally bite a small
piece out of the granite wall in front, losing a number of teeth
in the process, but until the great force operating in the north
succeeds in getting *across* the peninsula on the other side of
Achi Baba it is and must be stalemate.
'They have had very heavy fighting and I dare not mention
their losses, though no doubt those of the Turks have been
gigantic. Some day you will know that for the number engaged
this is far the bloodiest fighting of the whole war. . .

* Cheeseman, one of the young New College dons.

119

'My poor S. rifle and K. Scots Brigade* lost seventy officers and 1,300 men on the 28th June. You ask whether I have had a chance of using my division myself. Why, yes. On the 12th and 13th July the 52nd Division entirely alone, except of course for corps artillery, fought a very hard and trying engagement and took a very large group of Turkish trenches, *all* they were ordered to take except one small piece, and *held* all they gained, which everybody has not done. I can tell you—I confess the good God was very merciful and the Turks made no real counter-attack as we were so done and exhausted that we should certainly have lost some of the ground gained. The division lost a hundred officers and 2,800 men. The only recognition we have received was a telegram in *The Times* of 16th July saying "Part of the forces under my command attacked and captured, etc. etc."—not one word about the 52nd Division —and then to put the lid on was a statement that the RN Division was sent in to recover a trench that was lost. They were sent in late on the afternoon of the 13th to attempt to take the one trench that we had *not* captured. They never got near it, never retook anything, lost thirty officers and their attack was a complete failure. So is history in the newspapers written.

'I am getting old now and impervious and indifferent but the younger men feel and resent these mistakes. My division, as you will gather, has received a severe shaking which would try any of the best troops in the world. In France troops undergoing such a shock get a period of rest out of danger and receive reinforcements and refit. Here this is not possible as nowhere are you out of fire, and digging and fatigue work are continuous, and though I have received a lot of young officers from Scotland not one man has been sent me and new blood is most sorely needed.

'With one or two exceptions the division has pulled round well and we are again in the trenches, and have quite got the ascendancy over the Turk as regards bombing and sniping. Such experiences however must have their mark on second line

* Presumably the Scottish Rifles and King's Scottish Borderers.

troops. The Turk I think is a very clean fighter, recognises the red cross—and we hear today that eleven men of mine, missing on the 12th, as being in Constantinople all wounded and being well treated. Missing as a rule has meant dead.

'In my opinion the men who have done best here have been the City battalions, Glasgow keelies and Edinburgh clerks and Leith dockers. Miners too fight well. The Border and South of Scotland agriculturalist is good in parts but not up to the others. Give me the Glasgow corner boy with good officers.

'They are making preparations for a winter campaign here and are getting out designs for huts. The prospect is not pleasant—at present we are troglodytes, but the first rain, and it is not far distant, will drive us from our burrows. Oh, that Winston and his swollen-headed attack on the 17th March with ships alone! We should be in Constantinople now if we had attacked then with an adequate land force— such a force as we have now, not two divisions as they attempted it a month later.

'The health of the troops, *considering*, is not bad but diarrhoea is very prevalent and we have a great many off duty with it. Practically every shrapnel wound becomes septic but we have had only three or four cases of the invariably fatal "gas gangrene". There is enteric, but very little. The troops are well fed and get rice and dried fruit and raisins. The hospital arrangements here are good and the evacuation of the wounded very speedy. At first I fancy it was awful—one ship arrived at Alexandria with 400 wounded on board and one vet in charge! When I was at Alexandria in early June it was one vast lazaretto, so was Cairo.

'The last fortnight's fighting here (on 6th and 7th August) and to the north must have put a tremendous strain on the RAMC. I know the number of wounded that have passed into and through Mudros since the 8th but I must not mention it. . . . Please send any parcels or any goodies. All are welcome, even if one can't eat them oneself—as is my case at present. Half our parcels and packages however are stolen and looted— it is infamous—a parcel by *post* often takes six weeks from

England and if it bears the imprint of some purveyor of tobacco or groceries like Fortnum & Mason it often never arrives. By post, mind—not parcels by ships. They are nearly always looted. We want HE and shells however more than we want parcels' . . .

But the letters to me change during 1915; the dew of that early patriotism has dried away. I quote a 1915 letter from another Old Etonian. It begins by thanking me for a letter and shortbread,

'. . . both of which were extraordinarily acceptable in this almost uniquely loathsome part of the globe. I always said war was a mug's game and now I know it. I cannot conceive of any object, material or ideal, which would justify any sane man in undergoing such a combination of extreme danger and extreme physical discomfort. The regiment went into action about three weeks ago, leaving myself and four other officers in reserve at Lemnos, at which we (in our ignorance) groused. It was completely cut to pieces and when we arrived a week later we found that of the 360 men and ten officers 170 men and two officers remained. We found them in what was euphemistically called a rest camp which consisted of a large number of holes, some few hundred yards behind the trenches. During the two days after we arrived twenty-five men and four officers were laid out by shrapnel—one being killed horribly in the hole next to mine—and I came to the conclusion that my idea of a rest camp and the General's (who has now completely disappeared into the ground and is thought by this time to be somewhere near Athens) did not tally. . . I had some extraordinarily unpleasant escapes, one shell exploding on my seat in the officers mess about one minute before my occupation of it . . . I have a vast deal to say still on the subject of war but the flies make letter writing impossible and as I shall indubitably be killed before returning to England you will probably never hear it; which is a pity as it will probably aggravate you intensely.'

But was he killed in the end and if so, where? When do we meet again? Ned Grove, are you there?

Another letter from my friend Millicent at St Hilda's.

'We have just had very bad news. My dear brother Philip has been killed at the front . . . Nothing can make up for his loss, he was the dearest brother one could have. I know you will understand if I put off our tea party for the present . . .'

So it went on and there is one letter after another from Lewis Gielgud and quite a few from Aldous and Frances. There was this group: Aldous, Lewis, Gervas, Frances and me, always trying to get together and writing one another either long letters about everything or cheerful short scribbles, as so many of mine from Aldous are. Today we would have telephoned to one another, perhaps keeping in touch almost every day. But then it was letters and because of that something remains. Today's young groups will disperse as ours did and later on there will be nothing to remind them of the fun and worries and fears and plans and good ideas which they had. But there will be fewer ghosts, fewer letters to trap and bite their older selves, armoured by experience and yet still vulnerable.

XIII

St Thomas's Hospital

In 1915, with Dick away I became more and more impatient
with Oxford and my own non-involvement. Girls I knew had gone
to do 'war work'; one or two were even in munitions factories.
And at least I had passed first aid and home nursing examinations
and what was more Sister Morag Macmillan had chosen me as the
one to whom she could teach massage, feeling the hands of half a
dozen girls and rejecting them before taking me on. Whether she
knew I had some capacity as a healer which might be brought out
is something else again; had she sensed that she would wisely have
said nothing about it.

I nagged and nagged and finally went off to be a VAD nurse
at St Thomas's along with May Douie, an Oxford friend whom I
did not know very well. We stayed with the Hale Whites in Wimpole Street; he was one of the most distinguished and sympathetic
doctors of the period. Both were great friends of my parents and
related to the Douies. The Voluntary Aid Detachments of auxiliary
nurses had some kind of official status, though I am not quite
sure what, and was even less sure then. I had no idea what a
hospital was really like; I doubt if I had ever been inside one.
Our friends and relations would never find themselves in a hospital;
they went to nursing homes, especially the Acland at Oxford,
though there might well be arrangements there for almost free
treatment in certain cases. Some nursing homes or small, special
hospitals were quite well endowed. So St Thomas's was something
of a shock; the size, the long, clattering corridors and staircases
and the huge, undivided wards. Everything was, no doubt, sanitary,
but there were no frills.

We were worked very hard and it was a relief to come back to Wimpole Street in the evening. The Hale Whites' son, Leonard, had been in love with me; I can see this now from his letters. I had been very fond of him but had never thought of the possibility of his being hurt when I got engaged to Dick. And that again is now clear from the letters. No doubt he would have got over it. But his letters stop. As Tom Gillespie's stop. As Bey Gillespie's stop. As Geoff Wardley's stop. And as my brother-in-law Willie's stop.

So let me get away from the letters, back to St Thomas's: May and I, arriving on the early bus across Westminster Bridge, changing our shoes, hurrying off to our wards. It was difficult to learn that a nurse must hurry but never run. It was difficult to keep one's Sister Dora cap on straight. It was difficult to have to stand, even during sheet hemming (we were cheaper than sewing machines), when a doctor came into the ward, or for that matter a medical student one's own age or not much more.

I had brought the most interesting of the guinea pigs up with me and by special arrangement kept them in the animal house at the far end of the terrace along the river. They were, I think, an F2 generation and it was essential for our work on genetics to see how the offspring turned out. But visiting them was something else again, even though I did it in our nurses' dinner time, dashing away before the pudding, which was no great loss. But nurses were not allowed on the terrace, and once I was caught and severely reprimanded, though I tried to explain that this was part of a research project and might even have been approved by Florence Nightingale.

Unhappily one of the guinea pigs died. What was I to do? The Hale Whites' unperturbed parlour-maid told me: 'After dark, Miss, you take it out and put it into the middle of the street.' So I did and the Wimpole Street traffic disposed of the small body.

Of course May and I dodged the authorities if we possibly could. For years afterwards I thought of the boss class in the image of a hospital matron. However hard one had polished the brasses and the lockers it was never enough; we were always scolded, or at the very best ignored. We changed wards every week or fortnight but the routine was always the same: lavatories, bed pans, bottles, varied by floors and lockers. As we got more experienced there were temperatures and washing the patients. Once I was given some red paint for marking some bottles: I was even allowed to sit down for this. The beds had to be made exactly, the sheets squared and tucked in hard at the bottom with no regard for the patient's comfort. There was a great deal of sterilising to do; we were not immediately trusted with this. The wards were all the same, long rows of beds, perhaps thirty a side, each with a locker; a few patients could be out on the balconies with a view over the Thames, and the tiny figures on the terrace of the House of Commons, but most had nothing to distract them. No radio yet. Possibly a gramophone for an hour or two, when someone had time to wind it up. In the middle of the wards were, I think, the heating stoves and tables with sterilisers, heaps of sheets to be mended as well as any flowers which might be brought in; no room for them by the beds. Also in the medical wards there were usually one or two cots with small children. I cannot remember these children ever being visited by their parents. Probably at that time it was completely discouraged.

Of course I made awful mistakes. I had never done real manual household work; I had never used mops and polishes and disinfectants. I was very willing but clumsy. I was told to make tea but hadn't realised that tea must be made with boiling water. All that had been left to the servants.

Once when lifting a heavy patient my collar stud flew out and my stiff collar opened. Oh, dear! At that time we all wore stiff white cuffs, collar and belt into which we stuck our scissors, so much needed for bandages, dressings and sewing. One's blue skirt was ankle length with a long white apron over it. I ought to have had a proper uniform coat to go out in, but my mother had economised on that, thinking my own old one would do as well, but again I got an official scolding. We VADs waited in a crowd at the bus stop before Westminster Bridge; once a man spoke to me, but I turned away quickly and angrily and he saw his mistake.

Some of the wards were standard civilian patients, men or women, and often I couldn't understand their London accents, though I rather liked being called luv and ducks. There were always nephritis cases in great pain, usually terminal, with no treatment possible. I think the main pain-killer was still laudanum in some form. To combat sleeplessness, worry and any mental trouble or distress there were bromides and paraldehyde; I got to know the latter with its remarkably nasty and clinging smell only too well at the base hospital at Le Tréport where Dick, in the throes of hallucinations and some violence after his fractured skull in 1916, was regularly sedated with the nasty stuff. There were some effective purges and diuretics and of course bottles full of nicely coloured placebos. Anaesthetic techniques had made some advance, and surgery had gone a long way since the time of my broken leg seven years before.

The surgical wards with the real soldiers in their blue hospital coats, who had so lately come from the real trenches and the real war, were the most interesting for us. I write to Aunt Bay: 'They are much better fed than the civilian wards and there is scarcely any discipline; they sit on their beds and sing and smoke as much as they like.' Most had been treated first at dressing stations or base hospitals, then been sent on more or less cleaned up, but bad wounds had gone gangrenous and smelt awful. We VADs were put to help by holding dishes and so on during the hideously painful dressings, often with strong stinging antiseptics, when strong men whimpered or cried out: 'Hard,' as I wrote to Aunt Bay, 'to hold one's basin steady when a man is writhing about in his bed, white with pain and begging the nurse not to go on.' Here I disgraced myself once and once only by fainting. I was so scolded by Sister that I have never in my life done it again. However, as soon as I was allowed to help actively with the dressings I did all right. But becoming acquainted with all that pain did something so drastic that I had to write about it, to externalise it on to paper, in order to get it out of my mind:

127

hence the blood and pain in *The Conquered* and my earlier stories.

Probably by the summer of 1915 many of the best sisters and nurses from St Thomas's had been drafted off to base hospitals and ambulances; we VADs were the lowest of the low in the pecking order, and those who had been trodden on were happy to tread on us. We were seldom told what was wrong with the patients and the one and only Sister who did tell us and took some trouble to explain the treatment got increased loyalty and intelligent service. I was somewhat upset at being put into a VD ward and experienced a kind of moralising dislike for the patients, as well as being extra careful over sterilising basins and thermometers.

The other thing which I found upsetting was to see a patient with his eyes closed and throat heavily bandaged, with a policeman in full uniform sitting next to him. The patient was of course a suicide attempt and this was a crime. Was he arrested as soon as he was conscious? I never knew. Both disappeared from the ward. One thing missing was the blood transfusion apparatus which is now so common in an accident ward that one takes it for granted.

For many of the girls it was something of a shock to have so close an experience of naked male bodies, seldom beautiful. I had seen my brother more or less naked and handsome enough sufficiently often, though probably he had not seen as much of me under the usual family decency code. But whether I really ever had a full frontal view is something else again. A slight turning away or dropping of the eyes would have been the acceptable thing. But I don't remember being shocked by the soldiers I had to wash, only pitying, sometimes disgusted, usually matter of fact.

One of the servicemen with a leg wound had been a professional pickpocket. Even from his wheelchair he did marvellously, though we always got our scissors or hankies back from his locker. We dared him to get our wrist watches, and somehow he always managed it. One couldn't have advised him to take up any other profession. If by any chance he ever reads this, I would love to know how he got on.

There were a few air raids on or around London at this time, but so small by later standards that they seem irrelevant. We looked for Zeppelins on moonlit nights and once I thought I saw one. What I did see was the burst of flame when a gas main on the South Bank was hit, reflected splendidly in the river, and I remember the shaking of the heavy curtains in the drawing-room window at the Mitchisons' Chelsea Embankment house. But it was possible for some people to go on living quite an agreeable and often profitable life in many parts of Great Britain during World War One. That at least was barely so the next time.

The food at St Thomas's was awful, though I suppose better than hospital food a generation earlier. I thanked Aunt Bay wholeheartedly for her offer of cakes and chocolate: 'Most people do bring something extra for tea.' I still remember the dinner-time chunks of aged fish in batter. Finally there was milk from an infected farm and a number of us, myself included, went down with scarlet fever. This was then more serious than it is now; I was taken back to Oxford in an ambulance and put behind disinfectant-soaked sheets. A letter from Aldous in August 1915, thinking he had better not come to stay until my quarantine was over, dates this.

With even my short St Thomas's training I was snapped up to help with outpatients at the Radcliffe, which was very short staffed. These of course were the usual civilian patients, many children among them, often with small burns, cuts and so on. I would take off the dressings, clean up and then the Sister would inspect and probably tell me to get on with the same treatment. I think I did this reasonably well and became quick and expert at bandaging.

Meanwhile I started up my academic work again, rather half-heartedly, but I suppose I was persuaded into it, especially as I was too young to do VAD nursing in France. Frances was taking a degree, and I went to the same physiology lectures. I remember Professor Sherrington with his arm round the neck of a skeleton shark, looking affectionately at its rows of teeth.

There was also the soldiers' club in the High where I used to help, taking round tea, cutting sandwiches and so on. Heavy chaff went on, but always very decent by today's standards, no four-letter words, though I had heard a few in St Thomas's, usually from patients recovering after an anaesthetic. There was still a rather clear distinction between officers and men in general treatment, especially in convalescence. There were a number of small private hospitals in large houses given by individuals and with the running expenses partly at least paid by them, but mainly staffed by RAMC and other professionals. My parents-in-law offered Clock House on Chelsea Embankment as an officers' hospital which it duly became. They themselves were in the house next door. I expect treatment was as good as it was in the big hospitals; the consultants were much the same. Perhaps the young assistant nurses were rather prettier and more numerous, if sometimes less efficient. Cross-infection might have been less. But it was part of an amateur effort which did at least make people suppose they were all in it together and in so doing knocked some of the sharp edges off the class stratifications. One must also, I think, remember that some at least of those who made big amateur contributions, which really ate into their capital—and this certainly happened—in so doing helped on a bit of equalisation. For others it made absolutely no difference.

XIV

I would be different

It was not until three years after my marriage, when I was twenty-one, with a baby, that my mother took me to Coutts' to be introduced to the firm and open an account, with £250 a year, paid quarterly, half by the Trotter firm of Writers to the Signet, half by the Haldane firm. This was quite a lot of money in those days, though I spent it unwisely, in the excitement of having real money of my own. For instance, I got a beautiful white embroidered Chinese silk coat for evenings, out of which I must have shone. But at the time of my marriage I was still on pocket money, though it must have been quite generous, as I don't remember not buying books I wanted. And I expect I was taken to Coutts' in the Strand when we were in London and realised how different it was from the ordinary bank in Oxford. All Trotter lineage females, but not males, ought to bank at Coutts, thus commemorating an early nineteenth-century feud between the Coutts and Trotter families, which stipulated that no male Trotter should ever hold any position in the Bank! There was also, I think, some kind of marriage settlement drawn up by the family lawyers on both sides.

I did not indulge in the extravagance of a trousseau, but my mother insisted on supervising certain articles of lingerie. I had always worn flannel pyjamas, but it was explained that now I would need night-gowns and they must open in front. I knew why, but did not want to think about it, especially with her and the shop assistants looking at me. Also, because it was an early February wedding, these night-gowns must be wool. This wasn't easy; I felt the shop assistants being amused, and I got so upset by my mother's over-emotional approach to all this, that I burst into tears and rushed out of Debenham & Freebody.

From the old letters, it seems that there was some disapproval of the marriage taking place in 1916 from my in-laws, who perhaps felt that they might be left with this rather difficult young woman on their hands, possibly with a baby, should their son be killed. There was a distinct rift between the two mothers, with me, having decided that the marriage was going to happen, putting my not inconsiderable persuasive weight, both on the grown-ups and on Dick who, I think, found it all very embarrassing. I might so easily have been nicer to his parents. But I wasn't.

Nor did it help that I refused to be married in church or even to get a new dress. I wore the one Dick liked, black skirt—wool of course!—and a sleeveless black waistcoat top over a green silk shirt, and a felt hat kept on by hat pins with his regimental buttons as heads. That really upset Dick's mother who would probably have given me a gorgeous wedding dress with all the trimmings, if she'd had the least encouragement. By that time the war had gone into an austerity phase, especially for my mother and other sacrificers, so in the end there was no party, only a few close friends, including Aldous, asked to the registry office, and only a small wedding cake which we took to the soldiers' club where I had been working, and which was cut by me with Dick's cavalry sabre, the only use it was ever put to.

I had rather few wedding presents; my own young impecunious friends tended to give me books, though Rob Cross gave me a lovely Copenhagen china guinea pig, which I still cherish. The families produced some bits of silver and we put it all out in the school-room. I have many affectionate letters from this time and there were many, too, which my mother kept. Her dearest friend, Christian Fraser Tytler of Aldourie writes: '. . . It is everything that you should know Mr Mitchison as you do and that you can confide her life and happiness to his keeping with such absolute knowledge that he is worthy of such a trust.' Professor Alexander writes lovingly though a little teasingly. And there is a long and serious letter from Granniema at Cloan: 'Marriage is a momentous step, but the happiest when two hearts are joined in one and in determination to reach the fulfilment of the highest aims in life.' She goes on: 'My father proposed to my mother when she was sixteen and she was married at eighteen by her mother's wish for postponement, and certainly the fifty years (within a few months) they spent together were all that could be wished in happiness and perfect accord.' Being a true believer in freedom of conscience, she did not mind that I was not married in church.

As soon as the marriage was announced in the papers, a shower of advertisements came, including some for quite attractive clothes, including tea gowns, perhaps just too daring and immoral, in chiffon, brocade and lace, but also some remarkably ugly china, plate and so on. One was asked to favour firms with a visit to inspect their silver and gold fitted cases. I did in fact have a blue leather case with silk pockets and silver-mounted flasks, brush and comb with my initials, I expect from my nice, quiet father-in-law, but gradually everything got lost.

One could find suitable wedding presents, like a solid silver gadroon two-bottle ink-stand costing five pounds upwards, or a dinner service of Old Lavender pattern, 101 pieces for £8/7/6, or a toilet service including one chamber for as little as a guinea. There was little sign that we were in the middle of a war, except for one advertisement of military badge brooches, diamonds and enamel from seventeen pounds upwards, as well as wrist watches with luminous dials and hands, so that 'they can be seen on The Darkest Night'. And here are all these advertisements still, in one of the envelopes, as well as dozens of invitations from Court (and other) photographers to take my portrait with no obligation to buy, and others from florists wanting to do the church and reception and enclosing testimonials from the aristocracy.

None of this found its way to me during those few weeks in January, when I was thinking with increasing uneasiness and even alarm about the coming event, and the awful winter trench warfare went on, the duck boards over the sucking, stinking mud, the bodies of friends frozen onto the wire, tatters of uniform and human flesh. More of our twenty-year-old friends killed. I had a look at the Oxford registry office in the High, paid for the licence and a char to sweep down the stairs and passage, a total cost of fifteen shillings. So this was happening to me. I would be married and really grown-up. Everything would be different.

XV

The Pencil Diary

Well, there I was, a married woman, but still tied up with a host of attitudes, some of which I accepted, while others I questioned, but not enough to take really abrasive action. I was still treated as a young thing in need of protection. I was going on desultorily with bits of university education. Nothing to do with that, but I was also beginning to think on and off for myself. And our friends went on getting killed and I saw my father and mother both weeping for them. What was it all for? The younger people at least had begun to discount the patriotic rubbish which we had fed on at the beginning. I heard about the League of Nations Society. Surely that was an idea that made sense?

After our marriage leave we had another small one, which we spent at the Dalmally Hotel, where Dick went out fly-fishing, a highly skilled occupation with which I had little sympathy, though I tried to disguise this, always hoping that at some point he would catch a fish. I botanised happily, or drew bad plans of houses. Soon after this came the loss of the *Hampshire*; I was not at all unhappy that Kitchener was gone, considering how disastrously he had dealt with the gas mask situation the year before.

Some of the young men were now back at Oxford. Lewis Gielgud had been badly wounded and I felt a certain guilt at having egged him on into the army in the days of our early patriotic fervour. It did mean one saw something of them and got back for a short time into one's old world.

Lewis asked me to come to the May Day carols at Magdalen and then have breakfast. I looked forward to it tremendously; I would go down in my canoe, starting before dawn, crossing the rollers and paddling with the current and under the sweep of the young tender green. But then it appeared that this was unsuitable; I must have a chaperone; my mother would come with me. How could I say that this spoilt it all? Yet she must have known. I paddled from the stern of the canoe; she sat in the bows facing me in a thick grey coat; she looked pained and sad and perhaps she was. We had little conversation. And the young May leaves had lost their beauty and become flat paper. Lewis of course welcomed her with his usual excellent Etonian manners; nobody at that breakfast table was going to make a pass at me; we only wanted to be young together. The carols and the Morris dancing were as expected; I was aware that Magdalen on May morning was beautiful. But resentment came between all that and me. A nasty destructive emotion, as bad really as jealousy and as difficult, but equally important to get rid of.

My poor mother, who for so many people was a marvellous hostess, comforter, knowledgeable adviser, shoulder to cry on, in fact substitute parent, why had all this gone wrong between her and me? Are substitutes better than real parents? For some people and some purposes no doubt. My brother and I were perhaps the wrong children for her to have.

Meanwhile Dick had transferred to Signals. It was clear that there would be no more cavalry charges for the Queen's Bays. Instead he now had a motor-bike. They were just behind the lines in northern France. He was going to get three days leave and I was to join him in Paris; one went straight to Paris with no bother by train and boat. What fun it was going to be! My brother was around on leave or transfer and he and I went to a matinée in London; it was the Bing Boys and we enjoyed every moment; Gaby Deslys was dancing and Jack clearly found her luscious—as so many others did. Or was this another time? And someone sang *Another little drink* with the titillating lines about Asquith. I quote from memory:

In Parliament today when they get into a stew,
When they're all keyed up and don't know what to do,

Mr Asquith says in a manner sweet and calm
'Another little drink won't do us any harm.'

We went back in high spirits to the Mitchison house on the Embankment and there was a telegram. Dick had gone on his motor-bike on some errand for the Signals mess. At Gamache crossroads a French army car ran into him and left him for dead with the motor-bike on top and burning him. A British car which was following them picked him up unconscious and took him to the base hospital at Le Tréport. Here they found he had a fractured skull. The administrative wheels began to turn. I as next-of-kin was sent for; this was done in that war when possible for seriously wounded cases. His father came with me; it should have been a chance for him and me to get to know one another, but it didn't work out that way, which was a pity and mostly my fault. I kept a diary for this period which somewhat shows me up. It is written in pencil on a flimsy block of paper which I must have bought at Le Tréport, but is quite legible.

When I started it I was already extremely impatient with Dick's parents and yet felt guilty about my feelings towards them. The diary is very competently written with sharp and intelligent descriptions of people and places, and knowledge of myself trying to keep calm by thinking that now I knew how the heroine of a novel, which I was already trying to write, was going to feel. This habit of taking notes on one's own behaviour in periods of emotional stress is rather dangerous if people catch you at it.

At the beginning I was getting my main support from Jack (still called 'Boy' throughout). Here it starts, as we came back from the theatre to the house on the Embankment. When I was going back upstairs, my father-in-law

' . . . caught me by the wrist and half dragging me up to the stairs, said in a harsh and painful whisper "We've had a telegram. Dick is hurt." Then I, "How badly, my God, how badly?" "Very dangerous." I thought suddenly that he was breaking it to me that Dick was killed. "Give me the telegram. Where is he hurt?" "The head. Dangerously." I was in the dining-room by this time; Mrs M was sitting on a chair; she got up and kissed me and I thought to myself—the skull; probably he's dead now. And tried to remember about the respiratory centre and the vagus—suddenly all reality was sucked away from things and there was no way of telling whether I was dreaming or not. "Let me tell Boy," I said, but Mr M went to tell him leaving me and Mrs M in the dining-room: I still had the tune of one of the songs tinkling somewhere back in my mind; but the rest was completely a dream. I wanted Boy very badly. Mrs M was crying; she was all shrunk up and her emotion was catching at mine and breaking down my self-control. I looked at the telegram—dangerously ill—they wouldn't say that unless it was very bad indeed . . . Mr M came in, he was looking very old and both of them almost hopeless . . . I thought I should never see Dick again . . . Boy came in, and he was very calm and strong, but a little white and already thinking what to do . . . I felt very sick and clutched at the edge of the table and choked . . . I was being shaken by the certainty that Dick was dead; every few minutes I felt that suddenly and bit my hand but couldn't stop myself crying . . . the day went by and I can't remember exactly, only some things isolated . . . Boy alone with me in the dining-room when the crest of one of these waves of fear and longing for Dick caught me and I clutched at his arm with both hands and he was so perfectly and splendidly sane and spoke fairly sharply like cold water . . . and the queer feeling that I was acting and must do the thing expected of me in my part . . .'

Then there were all the arrangements to make and clearly I became reasonably calm and efficient and annoyed at the general assumption that I must be looked after. The night before we left, 'I dreamt that it would be all right and woke wondering whether that would be a good sign.' Goodbye to Jack and would I see him again before the end of the War—or then? We went down to Folkestone in a Pullman car—I for the first time—then embarkation, 'beautifully smoothly worked'. I looked about me.

'The lower deck of the boat was thick with soldiers, sitting or standing about, with their equipment and a haversack full of things. On the upper deck were officers—a lot of red tabs, and some French, sitting on ship's chairs, and a few like us, civvies, anxious looking. Everyone wore life belts, uncomfortable as they could be, but looking less stupid over khaki than over mufti . . . We started in half an hour or so, with a faint and not inspiring burst of cheering. A little spray came onto the decks; below a few of the men were singing *Michigan* and *Tipperary* spasmodically and with no great heart . . . I had recovered my *aequanimitas*, saying to myself: we shall find Dick better; in a little I shall be laughing at my fear now and wishing I had known that it was going to be all right, so as to be able to enjoy this crossing; therefore let me enjoy it now. I was also saying: if Dick is dead, what shall I do? I must have some plan; I think I shall take Greats or be a doctor . . . But still I was a little stunned and the clock of reality seemed to have stopped twenty hours before.

At Boulogne Dick's poor father fussed and tried to hurry things 'which was of course no earthly use. There was a crowd of RAMC people, a sturdy little woman, a canteen worker, very much pleased with her khaki, a tall, gaunt lady in black, dishevelled from the voyage, also trying to hurry her papers through . . . It was all very simple though; our things were not even looked at in the *douane*; an officer herded us through; we went off to a hotel in a car, Mr M hurrying me on when I wanted to change my money and then being late himself.'

By that time I had made friends with Mrs Johnstone, the dishevelled lady in black, whose boy was wounded in the leg and arm in hospital at Abbeville; she lent me a motor veil; one needed them in those days. Lunch was served by VADs in uniform—no doubt older than me, as one wasn't allowed out of the country until at least over twenty. The RAMC captain saw us into an official car and off we went through the cobbled streets of Boulogne, past a sentry onto a road with barley growing at each side, while the lady with the wounded son and I talked together, finding we were fellow Scots; the son was only twenty-one.

'I thought the harvest seemed very thin and poor; there were few boundaries and cattle grazed tethered . . . sometimes a girl, straight bodiced and barefoot, driving a cow; a few gleaners, old men and women, each with a ragged bundle of corn . . . villages with straggling houses, painted white or blue and usually an *estaminet* with the French soldiers in their pretty and unfamiliar horizon blue standing about. Along one stretch every village was full of zouaves, bronzed and handsome people with red fezes and baggy knickerbockers, who grinned at us as we went past bumping on the *pavé*, hooting wildly before corners . . .'

For we were driving at the unprecedented pace of fifty miles an hour with the wind beating and booming in our faces and ears.

After two tyre bursts, and my admiration for the RAMC chauffeur who changed wheels so quickly, we got to Abbeville and found the hospital where Mrs Johnstone's boy was, and waited.

'After a time the chauffeur came out saying, "That lady's had bad news; they say her son won't live." It depressed Mr M visibly but I thought it might be the natural delight in horrors —even after two years in France at war—of that class. And so it was, for after a long time she came out, more than ever dishevelled with her eyes bright, but saying he might have to have a leg off but would live. We left her things at the YMCA building in a little courtyard . . . It came on to rain, torrents all in a minute beating along the streets . . . we put up our canvas hood; I noticed how very many house pipes leaked.'

But by now I was worrying and wondering as we got nearer Le Tréport. I had

'. . . a picture in my mind: a long ward, just getting dark, a few yellowish lights along the walls, the evening grey outside; rows of white beds, a grave sister; red screens and two round one bed; inside a little light, on the pillow a head bandaged; eyes shut; perhaps a little muttering or a vague toss about of hands, not conscious life. I elaborate the picture; put in a basin or two on a locker by the bed—ice in a flannel bag—hear myself ask the sister how it goes—the watch through the night—'

About this time I began taking omens from the magpies in the fields. But Dick's father had no such irrational consolation. We got to Le Tréport and I put down every detail of the place. 'Suddenly I feel very queer.' We pulled up in front of the hospital, I jumped out and ran up the steps, asking the cheerful-looking RAMC sentry for Lieutenant Mitchison—Queen's Bays. 'Surely he would have known if there had been a death among the officers.' Then the doctor came, quite young, nice-looking, speaking to Mr Mitchison who seemed more upset than ever and couldn't speak. 'How is he?' I said. 'You are the wife, aren't you?' I nodded. He explained that Dick was slightly better, but the condition was still very dangerous. We went up three flights of white stone stairs, which I was to know very well. The hospital had been a grand hotel, as I write later 'the sort of hotel one has never been to oneself, bathrooms to every bedroom and landings one could dance on'.

'I wait outside, while Sister goes in, leaving the door ajar. Suddenly a voice, so strong and familiar I can hardly believe it. "What, my wife? Bring her in at once, Sister." I go in. It is a small white cheerful room, a bed with a silk quilt. Dick, looking very well and normal, but for a very unshaved chin: "Hullo Nou!" Sister leaves us for a few minutes. I try not to talk or let him, but he, talking rather too loud, asks questions, is very cheerful, moves his head about, is sorry he is such a wretched sight but he can't get his shaving things. There is a slight smell of paraldehyde . . .'

After that his father and I settled into the Hotel des Bains, 'a quaint place with a twisty stair . . . my room is small but has three windows that swing open like doors. One looks towards the *place* and the harbour with grey-sailed fishing boats, the other two onto a narrow street, very crowded in the evenings with poilus and their girls. I expect Mr M is writing letters in the salon or reading the Continental *Daily Mail*—a bad paper but with good news. His letters take three times as long to write as mine.'

At this point, we were going up to the hospital twice a day, though only I was allowed in.

'I see him every day for an hour or two . . . his head aches of course, very badly . . . I think it's a great pity they don't tell him more; as it is he is always trying to get up, even when I am there, and when I prevent him calls me all kinds of stupid fool, which I'm sure I am, but not for that. Mostly he is quite sensible, and even when delirious very rational, arranging a dinner party, talking about the Signal Troop or leave; he even wrote out a telegram to the Paris Hotel . . . The usual thing is five minutes normal though in pain, talking sensibly and not very restless; then a few minutes while the pain comes on, very restless, perhaps trying to get up, with his body and arms rigid, mouth open and eyes shut, cursing his headache or complaining of the pain, calling on himself to stop it, and then five minutes lying back, quite exhausted, often with one arm thrown over his forehead . . . His date memory has stopped the day of the accident; sometimes he asks how old I am . . . hearing all right, though eyes are not yet.'

I give a run-down on the doctors, who sound efficient and on the whole cheering, but my real praise is for Sister Holbeach, charming and sympathetic, 'not un-necessarily professional . . . as becomes a nurse, optimist'. I had told her about my nursing experience at St Thomas's and she said that she had spoken to Matron and I would be allowed to nurse Dick more of the time. What I don't say in the diary, and yet now I remember most vividly, is that, at the first interview, the doctor said he would probably not live, but conceded that he was in very good con-

dition and might recover. I know I dug my toes in about this;
it was just not going to happen; that is why I didn't put it into the
diary. When it didn't happen I was told that he would probably
never recover intellectually and might live in a somewhat crippled
condition. I expect they were quite sorry for this eighteen-year-
old, faced with a life sentence of this kind. But again, I refused to
believe it and that is why it isn't in the diary. I was fighting to win,
as Janet fought for Tam Lin.

Meanwhile I was taking in Le Tréport. By this time I was
reasonably fluent in French, and, from looking at a notebook I
kept for years with quotations in it, it is clear that I normally
read quite a lot of French poetry. So now I looked about me:

'The blue French soldiers in the streets are slightly more
untidy than their English *confrères*—a step nearer the battle-
field—many of them wearing one or two medals. I never can
tell the ranks apart. Some very fine horses . . . and there is
khaki among the blue, officers mostly, either RAMC or from
the regiments near here—come in mostly as far as I can see
for a drink and a bath, possibly for a little distracting society . . .
the ladies of the place are mostly bourgeoisie—a quantity of
flappers, less obvious and more subtle than the same type at,
say, Bournemouth . . . short skirts, bright coloured blouses
and caps or veils tied over their hair.'

There were families staying at the hotel.

'A very nice French colonel with grey moustache and grey
kind eyes; he has a boy of seventeen and one of about eight,
delicate looking, both of them . . . a young mother and a charming little girl of five or six with masses of yellow hair, blue
jersey and shorts and long bare legs . . . a good lady with hair
in a tight knob who has a horrid snivelling son in a tight
brown suit whom she is always looking after very carefully;
I think French boys of that sort of age are particularly horrible.
. . . at the *table d'hôte* a group of VADs in their blue caps,
cheerful and English, sometimes a single lady in a velvet

tamoshanter and a short coat edged with fur who looks incomplete without an officer . . . the hotel people are charming and friendly . . . but I find everybody's nice to me.'

We walked to the hospital every day through the middle of the market, and sometimes I bought a few flowers. There were 385 steps to the cliff top. 'We probably meet Mr and Mrs Sassoon, very Jewish, friendly and good folk, but somehow one cannot imagine her pearl necklace, which is probably extremely valuable, to be anything but rather a bad sham.' We filled in the day somehow; I still have two pottery animals I bought then. There was a shop which had about two dozen one-franc classics, which I bought; I read a lot of Guy de Maupassant at this time. But I daren't buy a copy of the *Vie Parisienne*, because Dick's father would be shocked. Clearly we get on dreadfully badly, and I realise that it is largely the generation gap, but that didn't help.

'He's very English (doesn't shake hands when I, as a Scot, would) and when some of Dick's superior officers came to find out how he was . . . he was very formal and a little nervous and, when one of Dick's Signal troop came to find out too, he tipped most adequately, but it was I who did the talking . . . I wonder how much I misjudge him and myself; it's partly shyness with him; I'm not shy in the same way.'

It was early September and sometimes there was a storm which made bathing more exciting. I bathed usually in the early mornings when there was no crowd and one could run down from the hotel.

'There are long flat shadows on sea and sand; the sun is bright but not hot and when one is knee-deep in the smooth grey water, rhythmically stirred by long slow ripples, it makes a pathway; but there is no-one to go with. I have a comic French bathing-dress with scarlet trimmings and two blue anchors on the collar.'

There was shopping, trying to get some silk to make silk

144

pyjamas for Dick. 'Sometime perhaps, I shall go into Eu, or walk along the beach to the rocks, but one wants someone to go with who will enjoy it in the same way.' But the days went by. Dick saw another specialist, Gordon Holmes, and was said to be out of danger. But the fight had to go on and was sometimes curious.

'Today for instance he didn't even know me. In the morning he had a long talk with me, calling me Lindsay—a Signalling Officer. I think he enjoyed it very much, for, by a curious coincidence, this Lindsay knew many people at Oxford, Willie for instance, and Joseph. He had known Heath [Heath had been killed earlier that year] and on his saying that he was the finest man he had known, he and Dick gripped hands. Dick also told him about his "missus" and her family and finally they shook hands and Lindsay went away promising to come back soon. A few minutes after, Dick called Sister to ask me to go to him, and when I was there told me what a nice man was this "Lindsay"—poor Lindsay who only existed for ten minutes. Then in the afternoon, after a sleep, Dick woke up to say that he was going off at once to East Hertford to contest the seat with Pemberton Billing. He sat up and was not put off long by my saying there was no need for him to go for a fortnight. Then, for I didn't want him to struggle to get up, I tried to make him remember where he was. "No," he said, "I'm in hospital at Bethnal Green; I must telephone to the other hospital; how did I get here? Please fetch my clothes, I must go to Hertford." I reminded him of who I was, but he was politely incredulous, a little surprised at my wearing his wife's rings. "Admit, nurse, that you have stolen them!" and utterly shocked—the picture of virtue!—at this strange nurse kissing him! "My good girl, I've never met you before; I quite like you, but I wish you'd go away." I couldn't stop him getting up, so I called the orderly and finally Sister who managed to quiet him, taking his orders about telephoning to Hertford with the greatest calm. Then, as she was going away, Dick remarked, "Oh Sister, will you please ask this nurse to go; I don't know her," implying that she wasn't a credit to any hospital. Exit me!'

Once we went up to the hospital and found a big convoy had come in and there was a correspondingly big evacuation of patients well enough to go back to Blighty.

'We found all the back part of the hall covered with stretchers, on each an officer in a brown blanket, a woolly cap, and labelled. Most of the MOs were there, giving orders, looking at the labels, bending over to talk to their patients. The Sassoon boy was there, also Major Cripps. A long string of ambulances, all driven by women, came up to the door, one by one. The first row were picked up one after another, two orderlies to a stretcher, with sometimes a man in front shifted so that they could get one out from behind, like a great game of patience. It all went wonderfully smoothly . . . The next day the Sassoons and Miss Cripps left, which I'm sorry for. We used to see the Sassoons every day up at the hospital . . . once I went in to see the boy—a typical young Eton Jew, who will probably get on in the world very well.'

But could this have been Siegfried?

I had gone swimming and walking with Miss Cripps; we said '*bon soir*' but disengaged ourselves from the poilus. Often there were a few officers in for two-day leave from the division near us.

'Two evenings ago, after dinner in the salon, Mr M was reading, I was playing patience. We heard three or four officers come in and begin talking to Madame . . . they wanted to know about bathing; then they began to talk to one another about some particular incident at Delville Wood. Finally I chucked my patience, got up and said I was going to give them chocolates; Mr M seemed somewhat surprised and said it would embarrass them. However I ran upstairs and came down with my chocolates and offered them; they were really pleased and began talking to me, all at once, and before Mr M came out of the salon—very shy—I knew their names and some of their histories, where they'd come from, what they'd been doing, and how very particularly pleased they were to get back to real dinners and beds and bathing . . . They were KSLI 5th Battalion . . . Last night about half a dozen came into the salon and started a conversation as soon as they possibly could. They were awful TGs* mostly, but they'd just come from fighting the Boche in Delville Wood . . . we had a long talk about Syndicalism . . .'

Another was an Australian ranker, who told me about holding a trench for thirty hours in an advanced position; he was recommended for the Military Cross.

I try to type them.

'They're all conscientious fatalists and they all try to talk about England or after the war, but always after a little you get back to shop. There was a Major and several others, also a nice little Canadian doctor up at the Hospital, whom we had seen several times before, and he was quite drunk; I think he often is: not a good thing for a doctor . . . Here am I, sitting on a table in the middle of the stuffy salon of a third-rate French hotel, being as charming as I can to an audience of TGs, all to give them the memory of a pleasant evening to take back to the trenches by Givenchy; that's why I wear pretty frocks and hats and do my hair just not anyhow, but to look nice; it's probably as much worth doing now as it ever will be again in my life. I would give a lot to be able to sing.'

At this time another specialist, Meyers, saw Dick, said he was to go to Netley Hospital, where most people with brain damage went, and apparently thought that ultimate mental recovery was only a matter of time. But, as I write, 'It's certainly rather disconcerting that he's still just as bad mentally.' I describe another incident:

* Temporary Gentlemen—who remembers that bit of class-slang?

147

'He gets violently angry with both me and the orderly when we stop him, calling us both dirty cads and damned liars; he also hits out like anything, and when the orderly has gone reproaches me bitterly for having called him, saying it's the sort of low thing I would do and often, which of course is the best thing, turning over and being offended till he falls asleep. But often I leave him to the orderly, particularly when he says *"Enlevez cette femme là, c'est la mienne, mais enlevez la."* And then as a parting shot when I'm going out "I don't ever want to see you again." He forgets all about it by next time, but I'm so afraid it will stay in some sort of distorted image in his subconscious memory. Yesterday morning he told me how the doctors and orderlies had lured him to an opium den and nearly killed him, but how he had fought them all.'

Clearly this was fairly exhausting, especially as one could not be quite certain about ultimate recovery. But I had a last evening with two VAD nurses, Miss Duval and Miss Tozer.

'We went off in a car to the Forêt d'Eu . . . the most lovely evening . . . the Forêt still full of wild flowers and very green . . . long stretches of slim tall beech trees, sudden rises among birch and chestnut with a steep white bank at the roadside, trailed over with honeysuckle, small roads under an arch of beeches and a deer leaping across, a clearing with a reaped cornfield and back through high woods of straight thin trees and the pink sunset blinking behind the stems like jewels. I don't know whether they were lovelier when it was growing dark or before, when you get broken patches of sunlight lying across the road and clear, sudden greens, almost spring-like. We stopped at a little farm, in the middle of the wood like a fairy tale, a square court-yard, an orchard of apple trees covered with small red fruit and the forest closing in all round. In the quiet of the wood we heard twigs snapping, a bird, a dog far off, and then listening closer, every few seconds a thud, less sound than vibration, as if the earth were snoring a long way under, and that is the guns. When the wind is right they are quite loud and on dark nights they see from the hospital the horizon all lit with flashes.

'We had a perfect French dinner, omelette, chicken, haricot beans stewed in milk, cider, jelly and cream and bowls of thick soft coffee. And we all told one another our life histories and made friends and deplored the badness of a girl's schooling and how hard it is for her to make her way to any really educated work. Both the girls are scientists . . . it seems an awful waste that they should be VADs here in the position of privates under sisters who may or may not be nice, but anyhow discourage questioning and are very jealous. No chance of rising from the ranks or learning any more than they know now. They work for a twelve and a half hours' day, with three hours off and short meal times; once in two months they get a whole day off and once in eighteen months a week's leave. They're both going to chuck it when their terms are up and I think they'll be quite right.

'They were telling me one thing which must be particularly annoying to Miss Tozer, who was doing brain research before the war—that there are any amount of splendid head cases here which die, and it would be the chance of a century if there was anyone here to note symptoms and do a PM. Of course if she were to suggest such a thing—which she could probably do perfectly—the authorities would first faint and then kick her out. But it is stupid.'

So there was the magic again, but also the proper concern of the scientist. Miss Tozer, Miss Tozer, what happened to you? I looked you up in *Who's Who* just in case, but as we agreed, it is so hard for a girl to get up to the top—if that *is* the top.

We left the next day. There had been no more forty-eight hour leave people. But plenty of rumours. I add, 'Poor old Dick will be sick if the cavalry, as seems likely, get through in three weeks.' So, apparently, we thought!

There the pencil diary ends, with only a few more guilt feelings about my father-in-law. Typically, I never managed to arrive at what to call either him or Dick's mother. I couldn't think of them as parents and they were the wrong generation for first names.

So there we were, waiting very anxiously in London, where it had somehow been arranged that, before going to Netley, Dick should come to the Clock House hospital. It seems odd that these private arrangements could have been not only possible, but were not disapproved of. One only asks oneself whether the treatment of wounded officers was very different from that given to ordinary private soldiers. That wasn't a question I had asked, so far. One took certain things for granted. But Dick's parents and I were all in a rather agitated state, totally unsure of how he would be.

But something very odd had happened. For three weeks Dick had been in a strange country, usually in a hurry with something important he had to do. Sometimes he met people he knew, but often he was alone, or chased by non-human entities. Then he was on a boat in mid-channel and there were creatures crawling about the decks, sea snakes and whatnot. Then 'something clicked,' and he was back in the ordinary world, gradually realising where he was and why. And that was how he was when he came to us in London, very weak, but himself. He never quite recovered his sense of smell, though this is never strong with fairly heavy smokers as he was. But smell is supposed to come into taste, especially of wine, and this never left him. And quite soon he stopped being able to draw maps of the strange country.

XVI

War Marriage

Tough Dick got well quickly. The only sad thing was that he had forgotten that Geoff Wardley, his dearest friend, had been killed just before his accident. I had to tell him. He had a longish sick leave, during which he passed his Bar Finals exam; he had worried in case the exam-passing capacity had been damaged, but no. Once we were ragging around—it was at Aunt Kate's country house in Surrey—and he pretended to have gone mad; I was sitting on the back of a sofa and fell off, screaming with terror.

In late autumn we were up in Scotland in a huge house which couldn't let itself or its shooting during the war, so I suppose we got it very cheap. It was large and a little frightening. Dick gave me a gun and taught me to shoot, but I was never sure if I liked it, though I loved the dark woods and the crisp frost underfoot, and above all enjoyed my sporting costume—high boots and a short skirt. He tried to teach me proper games too, like chess, but I would always rather have been playing hide-and-seek or sardines, or some dressing-up game. But there weren't any other people to play with us. I made myself lists of improving books which I thought I ought to read, and stuck hopelessly in only too many classics. I went on writing verse.

At the end of his sick leave Dick applied for the Staff College and was accepted. He felt a bit guilty about this; it seemed like a way out of the real thing. There was always a certain amount of jeering at the red tabs. But I wanted him to be safe. How I wanted it! I loved and cherished him but there was an aspect that was not going well. We spent early 1917 in digs at Houghton Regis near Dunstable, where I was rather unhappy and not very well, for I was running a mild temperature every day. No doubt I was given tonics but they had no effect. This unhappiness would today have been rapidly sorted out and put right by any competent doctor or clinic. Or if I could have brought myself to talk straight-forwardly to Dick he would surely have understood. But no, no, I couldn't. In some way it must, I felt, be my fault. I don't quite know what the Staff course was, but Dick was away all day. I used to go for walks, but chalk country always scares me and it was a long cold winter with few flowers. In the evenings the batman came and Dick and I had hot saucer baths in the bedroom which slightly brought up the temperature.

Food got gradually worse; by the beginning of 1918 we were on to ration cards, which was a good thing, as there had been, earlier, food shortages here or there, and quite a lot of food profiteering. My father was always upset if my mother managed to get him something a little special, especially for his midnight cake—though the milk went on. If there was anything, he always wanted me to have it. But I got a special ration card as a nursing mother as soon as my baby was born. At the same time we were put on to 'standard bread', though that was made very palatable later on in the year, because there was a splendid walnut crop at Oxford. But we had very little idea of how nearly successful the German blockade was being.

In March 1917 news of the Russian Revolution came through, but we thought of it mainly from the point of view of how it might affect us and whether it would help to bring the war to an end. Lewis, back in London at the War Office, with his wound still giving him trouble, wrote in considerable worry; on the Gielgud side, he had a good dose of Polish patriotism and he felt, not without reason, that Poland would suffer.

News still had to be dug out of newspapers. People did not normally communicate by telephone and a telegram still tended to be bad news. The telegraph boy with his orange envelope was the usual dark angel. Willie was killed on September 20th 1917; his father wrote me a very sweet letter, not mentioning his own pain.

It was perfectly possible for a letter to arrive at Oxford by the morning post. Read at the breakfast table and reasonably promptly answered, the reply would get to London by the last post. The penny post, of course, and very dependable it was.

Dick went back to France in summer 1917, to a Staff post. We wrote to one another every day and went on doing this during the whole of our marriage, unless at times when either of us was in a place without regular posts; for instance when I was in India or Botswana, letters might be spaced to two or three days. Even if the other one could be at their most maddening—as all husbands and wives are bound to be in a day-to-day, live situation—there was the feeling that the other one was there: a permanent area of trust and confidence. This kind of relationship has little to do with romantic love; it can develop just as strongly in an arranged marriage. I still find myself arranging the words to describe a view, a flower, a political situation, so as to put it into my next letter to Dick.

It was after Dick went back, but perhaps when I was staying with his parents, that I got in touch with the headquarters of the League of Nations Society. The then secretary, Margery Spring-Rice, remembers me coming with a silent duenna, perhaps my mother-in-law's personal maid. I don't remember her; such people were only a mild nuisance and didn't count, nor would they comment on what had been going on. But I know I came away convinced, and with masses of literature, and after that I had to do something about it. How and where? Not in undergraduate papers. Not the Home Student *Fritillary*, which was used to publishing my poems. No, I was intent on bigger game. The *Oxford Times*.

I had never written for a newspaper and my first letters on the need for a supernational authority took me hours to construct. I did not think it was sensible to sign my own name; everyone would know I was only a girl even if I was married. So I signed them 'Mother of Seven', 'Returned Serviceman' and so on. For two or three issues I argued with myself; the then Editor of the *Oxford Times* must have been very sympathetic. But then the big names came in, Gilbert Murray, Ernest Barker and so on.

The Oxford branch of the League of Nations Society got off to a splendid start. I gave up in December; I was expecting my first baby in February and it was being taken very seriously. Owing to my riding accident at nine I had a somewhat twisted pelvis which was liable to make birth more difficult. I had various measurements and tests done and at the end of December I suddenly had a slight haemorrhage. I was put to bed and fussed over and in fact I was rather frightened, though Dr Carew Hunt, the very nice woman doctor who was looking after me, was reassuring.

Meanwhile an enormous layette had been bought: binders, long clothes—that is to say long flannel robes bound with silk to tuck in over the baby's toes. There were long dresses to go with this, cotton or silk, as well as two nineteenth-century family robes for best. Nappies were soft with the towelling one to the outside. There were no waterproof pants for babies (or anyone else) as yet, but possibly this was better for the babies. I had a rocking cot trimmed with muslin and ribbons and a baby's basket with soft towel and powder and all manner of baby requisites. I am sure Dick's mother gave me many presents of this kind.

I regarded all this with some dubiety. Certainly it was all very right and proper that I was going to have a baby and the interest and excitement I was arousing seemed all right and indeed my due. It would be dangerous and painful but that made it all the more interesting. But would I like the baby or at any rate would I like it as much as I was supposed to?

Well, dangerous and painful it was. I had plenty of lovely chloroform but even so it was worse than I had imagined possible. I must have had some infection which would have been speedily dealt with at a later stage either by sulfonamides or antibiotics. But at this period all that could be used must have been antiseptic douches. I took against the monthly nurse who had appeared in some alarming form while I was mildly delirious. However, the good old *vis medicatrix naturae* worked and the baby was after all surprising and delightful.

154

Maya was in her glory. I suppose she would have liked a larger family herself—in some ways. But it was really, I think, that she was now in charge of an important event on the same status level as the doctor, considerably higher than the nurse. I was entirely a novice and could be made to do the right thing. At this period it meant a diet with no fruit as that would 'sour the milk' and this was a real hardship for me. In addition I had lost such freedom as I had; I was once more liable to do the wrong thing and incur displeasure or see it put right in such a way that I felt stupid and incompetent.

1918 was a bad year because events seemed to have stuck, at least those which got into the papers. There was a choking weight on everything. Dick's first Staff job was in France; later he was moved to Italy. He got leave in summer and came over in the same boat as the Spanish 'flu. He went down with it and so did I but the baby, Geoff, called for Geoff Wardley killed in 1916, whom I was nursing, was untouched. But we spent a few rather miserable days in bed with high temperatures while Dr Carew Hunt puzzled about what it could be and the sunshine and garden scents wheeled round outside. At least he had seen his son, though I don't think he quite knew what his attitude was or should be. But we were lucky to have had some immunisation, for by that winter the 'flu was a killer.

There was still plenty of household help so I was free of the ordinary baby chores and Maya was always bathing him and hanging over us supervising. In fact I was married, but I had scarcely begun to be free, and I was being somewhat conditioned into not wanting this. When I had a house of my own, I was told, I would have to engage (and dismiss) servants, order food, see that everything was just so. But somehow I did not at all like the idea of all that and the one person from whom I couldn't learn it was my mother—or, I suppose, my mother-in-law. Nor would I have accepted, say, a domestic science course if it had been suggested from above. How stupid can one be! And yet perhaps I was clinging on to some part of me that had to grow but only on its own.

Frances meanwhile had got away. She, like me, had wanted to do war work, so after getting through her Science degree she went off to a hospital and worked as an anaesthetist. She had managed to get to Garsington but found it too full of distinguished and much older people asking sudden embarrassing questions. But I never got to Garsington. Nor did I as yet have any kind of regular or adequate allowance though no doubt I could have the (first class) fare to London if I was taking my baby to see his other grandparents. Yet already I sensed a jealousy, which was to become more marked later, growing up between the two grandmothers.

The longing to get away which somehow I was too incompetent or inhibited to put into action came through in verse:

> Tonight, if I was free, I'd go
> Out of the house, into the rain,
> Because the clock ticks here so slow:
> Down to the station—to a train,
> And get somewhere, away, away,
> Oh anywhere, but not to stay
> In this same place, day after day,
> And from the school-room windows see
> The branches of the walnut sway
> Across the garden: oh dear me,
> If only I could get away.

What worried me, I remember about this, was that the trees which I saw swaying in the North Oxford wind were not walnuts but elms. Elm-tree would scan, but not so well, not right somehow. And there were walnuts, splendid big ones, at the far end of the garden, though not to be seen from the west-facing window. So I borrowed them.

I did at least manage one escape. It was right at the end of the war, though of course it didn't seem like that to most of us in October 1918. I felt as if everything was going to go on for ever. But Dick found he could get leave and arranged for me to come out. This seems an extraordinary thing to us now, with our experience of more total war, but nobody found it strange at that time. I was all the more anxious to come because I had just read Marie Stopes's *Married Love* which seemed to me to have the answers to some of my own troubles if Dick too would read it and put some of it into practice. This was the first serious sex-instruction book for my generation and must have made an immense difference to the happiness and well-being of thousands of couples.

Dick was acting as *Officier de Liaison* between the French and British armies in northern Italy. They had been for some time in rather a static position so that most of what he was doing was foraging for the officers' mess, shopping, and doing things like explaining to a senior French officer that the Order of the Bath ('*Un bain—vaut mieux qu'un saint, quoi?*') was really quite important. He could get leave and we would spend it well behind the lines in Perugia. I could go via Paris. There were plenty of trains still running and no bother about getting tickets this end, nor did one even need a passport. But my parents and parents-in-law got together on the impossibility of my doing this journey alone, not so much for the physical danger which was not great in pre-air-warfare days, but for the moral dangers which they apparently could see all over the place.

I protested and sulked and tried to get round them in various ways. But they insisted on finding a chaperone who'd look after me on the journey to Paris, see me through that abode of wicked-ness and put me into the sleeper for Italy. We were introduced at Victoria Station; I said nothing but decided that this would not do. We were of course going first class; I suspect that they had paid for the good lady's ticket. On the boat crossing to Dieppe I seized my suitcase and plunged into the third class which struck me as much nicer as well as being so crowded that I could easily get lost. Luckily it was a very rough crossing. I take it that my chaperone was laid out; I never saw her again.

I enjoyed every moment. The train was so crowded that she couldn't have looked for me; in fact it was so crowded that, as I still remember vividly, I couldn't get along to the loo or rather I was too inhibited by some of this lady thing to push through with sufficient vigour. I took a taxi from one station to the other and duly got my sleeper. I felt suddenly and gorgeously free and grown-up. This time I'd really escaped and by my own wits. I had only twice before been 'abroad', once to Le Tréport and, earlier, once to Paris, always looked after. I talked to everyone I saw and told them all about going to see my husband. Later I recognised that there had been some slight attempt at getting off with me which I hadn't even understood. I would probably have been rather shocked if it had got through to me but I expect I looked very young.

It was terribly exciting going through the Simplon tunnel and coming out at the far end with Italy spread below one. This sense of a new country is something one misses entirely when one only arrives at another international airport. I leant against the window watching everything. I knew where I had to change and when I got out, perhaps at Milan, I simply used my main Italian phrase, '*Dove è il* RTO?' I was at once taken to the railway transport officer and carefully looked after as befitted the wife of a major. I got to Perugia ahead of Dick, found my way to the hotel but only just ventured out into the street, feeling that it was incredibly daring to be by oneself among a lot of Italians.

Then Dick turned up and we had a lovely time; I found to my delight that Italian pastry cooks were apparently not rationed on sugar; by that time I was really sugar-hungry and laid into cakes and biscuits. But on the last day or so a telegram came recalling Dick. It was the final push of October 1918. Following it came a telegram from his parents or mine—I can't remember which—telling me to return immediately. Dick saw me on to the train and rushed back to his division. We just didn't know what was going to happen.

But when I got as far as Paris I somehow met up with various old friends, including Lewis Gielgud and Gervas Huxley, who persuaded me not unwillingly to stay. I had enough money and they must have found me an hotel room. The three of us walked round the Place de la Concorde heaped with captured guns and cannon, a real old triumph, and the statues of Metz and Strasbourg garlanded with roses and chrysanthemums and the French crowds tossing with glory and excitement. But then I went down with the Spanish 'flu and spent two days in the hotel feeling rather ill. This was the 'flu which had killed or was going to kill many of my friends, but as I had managed to have it in the first wave this second attack was not too bad. There may have been another telegram and at any rate I felt I must go back.

I was in Oxford for the day of the Armistice. I remember buying a paper, jumping on to a bus in a state of almost hysterical excitement and half shouting at everyone else, 'The Armistice is signed!'

'Oh, indeed,' the lady on the opposite seat politely answered.